A CITIZEN'S GUIDE TO ENVIRONMENTAL ADVOCACY IN DELAWARE

KENNETH T. KRISTL, ESQ.
Professor of Law & Director,
Environmental and Natural Resources Law Clinic
Widener University Delaware Law School

Prepared pursuant to a generous grant from
The Inland Bays Foundation's
Austin/Moyer Citizen Advocacy Project

Published by H Watson LLC
as the first project of the Inland Bays Foundation
Austin/Moyer Citizens Advocacy Program

Cover design by Raeanne Hytone

ISBN # 978-1-946228-37-6

INTRODUCTION

I wrote this Citizen's Guide to assist citizens of Delaware who want to advocate effectively about environmental issues and concerns. The Guide seeks to provide general information and advice that will help Delaware citizens understand how the process works and ways to craft a message that can affect the decisions that give rise to those concerns.

The focus of this Guide is the State of Delaware's processes for making decisions about environmental issues. While there are other processes and actors that play a role in some decisions (for example, county zoning processes), they are beyond the scope of this Guide. While it does not cover everything, a significant volume of environmental decision-making happens at the state level. As a result, understanding how the state processes work, the general details of where, when, and how you can participate, and some strategies for making that participation as impactful as possible—the goal of this Guide—can help citizens be effective advocates for their environment.

This Guide consists of four chapters that serve two distinct roles. Chapters 1 and 2 describe how the state environmental processes work. This includes a general overview of how the Delaware Department of Natural Resources and Environmental Control, or DNREC, operates, the main programs that DNREC oversees and the environmental decision-making processes in those programs, and the procedures for public participation in the decision-making process. Chapters 3 and 4 focus on suggestions for how to advocate effectively within those Delaware processes.

Given the scope of this effort, I designed the Guide to provide general information so that citizens can understand. It is not, and should not be viewed as, legal advice. When dealing with a particular situation, you should consider consulting an attorney (especially if it involves appeals or other legal processes). Nevertheless, I hope the Guide helps you understand the processes so that you can ask an attorney informed questions and have a sense of how the process will work.

I want to thank the Inland Bays Foundation for asking me to undertake this project as part of their John Austin-Bill Moyer Citizen Advocacy Program. Having worked with John and Bill—who were very effective citizen environmental advocates themselves—it is an honor to undertake this effort to inform citizens and encourage effective advocacy. I hope this guide lives up to their legacy.

Professor Kenneth T. Kristl, Esq.
Professor of Law
Director, Environmental & Natural Resources Law Clinic
Widener University Delaware Law School

ABOUT THE ENVIRONMENTAL & NATURAL RESOURCES LAW CLINIC

The Environmental & Natural Resources Law Clinic is the fourth oldest environmental law clinic in the country, having served clients in Delaware, Pennsylvania, and throughout the Mid-Atlantic region since 1989. The Clinic is housed at the Widener University Delaware Law School's Wilmington, DE campus. The Clinic's Director, Professor Kenneth Kristl, is licensed to practice law in Delaware, Pennsylvania, and Illinois.

The Clinic exists to provide Delaware Law School students with the unique educational experience of representing real clients in real cases so that students can "learn by doing" and thereby prepare themselves to practice law after graduation. The educational experience of each student is closely supervised by the Clinic Director, who seeks out representations that will help fulfill this important educational mission. The balance sought is reflected in the Clinic's motto: "Preparing to Practice while Protecting the Planet."

The Clinic represents organizations that are formally created corporations and partnerships, organizations that are formed for a specific purpose but have not yet been incorporated, and individuals in environmental matters. Such matters can include permitting decisions (the focus of this Guide), changes to regulations and statutes, educational projects (like the preparation of this Guide), and the formulation of strategies concerning pending environmental proceedings. The Clinic has represented clients on matters under the federal Clean Water and Clean Air Acts, the federal Administrative Procedures Act, and numerous state environmental laws.

Historically, the Clinic has represented clients in federal courts (including the United States Circuit Courts of Appeal for the D.C. Circuit and the Second, Third and Eleventh Circuits), federal district courts (including the Districts of Delaware, Eastern, Central, and Western Districts of Pennsylvania, District of West Virginia, and the District of Puerto Rico), and state courts and administrative agencies. In Delaware, the Clinic has represented clients in the Delaware Supreme

Court, the Superior and Chancery Courts, and before the Coastal Zone Industrial Control Board and the Environmental Appeals Board. It has also represented clients seeking legislative changes in the Delaware General Assembly. In Pennsylvania, the Clinic has represented clients before the Pennsylvania Supreme Court, the Commonwealth Court, the Environmental Hearing Board and the Environmental Quality Board.

Persons seeking the Clinic's assistance with an environmental matter should contact the Clinic Director:

Professor Kenneth T. Kristl, Esq.
Environmental & Natural Resources Law Clinic
Widener University Delaware Law School
4601 Concord Pike
Wilmington, DE 19803
(302) 477-2053
ktkristl@widener.edu

The Clinic Director screens requests for assistance based on: (1) current capacity of the Clinic to take on the matter; (2) the educational opportunities for Clinic interns presented by the potential representation; (3) whether the representation promotes or protects positive environmental values; and (4) other factors, including whether the Clinic has the expertise to handle the matter, whether other attorneys are already representing the parties or interests seeking the Clinic's help, and whether the representation involves or requires the Clinic to seek monetary damages as part of the relief for the potential client.

TABLE OF CONTENTS

GLOSSARY OF TERMS

Clean Air Act (CAA)	The federal statute, found at 42 U.S.C. §§ 7401 – 7671q, which governs emissions of air pollutants
Clean Water Act (CWA)	The federal statute, found at 33 U.S.C. §§ 1251 – 1387, that regulates water pollution
Conversion Permit	A Permit under the CZA that allows new heavy industry or Bulk Product Transfer Facilities on 14 sites in the Coastal Zone
CZA	The Delaware Coastal Zone Act, 7 Del. C. § 7001
CZA Permit	A Permit under the CZA
CZICB	The Coastal Zone Industrial Control Board, which hears appeals of actions by the Secretary under the CZA
DNREC	The Delaware Department of Natural Resources and Environmental Control, the primary regulator and enforcer of environmental laws in the State of Delaware
EAB	The Environmental Appeals Board, which hears appeals of all Secretary's Orders except those under the CZA
FOIA	Freedom of Information Act, found at 29 Del. C. § 10001, which gives the public the right to obtain public records from state agencies. (There is a separate federal FOIA)
HAPs	Hazardous Air Pollutants

Hearing Officer	A person appointed by the Secretary to conduct a public hearing on a permit request and provide a recommendation for the action the Secretary should take
Hearing Officer Report	A written recommendation to the Secretary, prepared by the Hearing Officer after a public hearing has been held
NAAQS	National Ambient Air Quality Standards developed under the CAA
NEPA	The federal National Environmental Policy Act, 42 U.S.C. §§ 4321 – 4370h
NESHAPs	National Emission Standards for Hazardous Air Pollutants, developed under the CAA
Non-point Source	A source of pollution that does not meet the definition of a "point source" under the CWA
NSPS	National Source Performance Standards, developed under the CAA
NPDES	The National Pollution Discharge Elimination System permitting system created under the CWA. Permits regulating pollution discharge issued under the CWA are called NPDES Permits
Point Source	A discernible, confined and discrete conveyance, including but not limited to any pipe, ditch, channel, tunnel, conduit, well, discrete fissure, container, rolling stock, concentrated animal feeding operation, or vessel or other floating craft, from which pollutants are or may be discharged. Point sources discharges

are often regulated under the CWA and therefore require an NPDES Permit

Status Decision A decision by the DNREC Secretary under the CZA to determine whether a proposed project is not covered by the CZA, is covered and prohibited, or is covered and requires a CZA Permit

Secretary's Order A formal order issued by the Secretary of DNREC announcing and explaining his/her decision on a permit request or other formal DNREC action.

Subaqueous Lands Submerged lands and tidelands that are regulated under Delaware's Subaqueous Lands Act, 7 Del. C. § 7201

TMDL Total Maximum Daily Load, a restriction of the total amount of a particular pollutant that can be discharged by all sources into a waterbody that is considered "impaired" by that pollutant so that the waterbody's water quality will eventually improve.

TRM Technical Response Memorandum, usually prepared by DNREC staff at the request of a Hearing Officer, designed to have DNREC staff address issues raised at the public hearing or in public comments

US Army Corps of Engineers The federal agency that regulates activities in wetlands under Section 404 of the CWA

US Environmental Protection Agency — The federal agency primarily responsible for implementation of federal environmental laws

WQS — Water Quality Standards developed and promulgated under the CWA

CHAPTER 1
DELAWARE'S ENVIRONMENTAL REGULATORY STRUCTURE

In Delaware, environmental regulation occurs via an extensive statutory scheme set out over 69 Chapters in Title 7 of the Delaware Code[1] and the regulations promulgated pursuant to that statutory authority.

1-1. DNREC Is The Primary Environmental Regulator

Title 7 of the Delaware Code is entitled "Conservation." At least 39 of the 69 Title 7 Chapters empower DNREC to engage in some kind of environmental regulatory activity. These include:

Chapter 1 – Protected Wildlife
Chapter 5 – Licensing re Hunting, Trapping, Fishing
Chapter 6 – Endangered Species
Chapters 9, 11 – Fin Fishing
Chapter 13 – Enforcement of Game and Fish Laws
Chapter 17 – Dogs
Chapter 18 – Eel Fishing
Chapters 19 – 28 – Shellfish
Chapter 38 – Giant Reed Grass Control
Chapter 39 – Soil and Water Conservation Districts
Chapter 40 – Erosion and Sedimentation Control
Chapter 42 – Dam Safety
Chapter 45 – Public Lands
Chapter 47 – State Parks
Chapter 60 – Environmental Control
Chapter 61 – Minerals in Submerged Lands
Chapter 62 – Oil Pollution Liability

---

[1] You can find Title 7 of the Delaware Code at https://delcode.delaware.gov/title7/index.shtml#TopOfPage. This will take you to a webpage showing each of the Chapters in Title 7; you can click on a chapter title to see either a list of sub-chapters (clicking on a sub chapter takes you the statutory language) or the statutory language of the Chapter itself. The Chapters are not consecutively numbered; thus, you will find chapters numbers 70 and above even though the total number of chapters is 69.

Chapter 63 – Hazardous Waste Management
Chapter 66 – Wetlands
Chapter 67 – Motor Vehicle Emissions
Chapter 68 – Beach Preservation
Chapter 70 – Coastal Zone Act
Chapter 71 – Noise Control and Abatement
Chapter 72 – Subaqueous Lands
Chapter 74 – Underground Storage Tanks
Chapter 74A – Aboveground Storage Tanks
Chapter 77 – Extremely Hazardous Substances Risk Management
Chapter 78 – Pollution Prevention
Chapter 91 – Hazardous Substance Cleanup

Thus, for the vast majority of environmental issues, DNREC will be the first place to look for environmental regulation and protection.

The current configuration of DNREC identifies three main structural components within the Department:

Office of the Secretary, which includes a Division of Community Affairs and Environmental Finance Office;

Office of Environmental Protection, which includes the Division of Air Quality, Division of Waste and Hazardous Substances, Division of Water, and Division of Climate, Coastal, and Energy; and

Office of Natural Resources, which includes the Division of Fish and Wildlife, Division of Parks and Recreation, and the Division of Watershed Stewardship.

The DNREC website, particularly https://dnrec.alpha.delaware.gov/divisions/, provides description for these different Offices and Divisions.[2] This configuration

[2] You can also find the regulations relevant to the different offices at https://dnrec.alpha.delaware.gov/dnrec-regulations/.

suggests specialization: if you are interested in an air pollution issue, for example, you are likely going to see the Division of Air Quality dealing with it. Understanding this structure can help you determine where to direct your efforts.

1-2. DNREC's Authority In Major Areas of Environmental Law

As the long list of different Title 7 chapters above proves, DNREC has many different regulatory jobs. It is beyond the scope of this Guide to get into every one of those statutes. Instead, the Guide will focus on some main areas of regulatory concern handled by DNREC.

1-2.1. Water Resources

DNREC gets its regulatory power over water resources from 7 Del. C. § 6003(a)(2), which prohibits persons from undertaking "any activity . . . In a way which may cause or contribute to discharge of a pollutant into any surface or ground water" unless they have a permit from the Secretary, and 7 Del. C. § 6003(a)(3), which prohibits undertaking activity "In a way which may cause or contribute to withdrawal of ground water or surface water or both" without a DNREC permit.

As this statutory language makes clear, when thinking about the regulation of water resources in Delaware, it helps to classify those resources into two distinct groups: *Surface Waters* (that is, waters found on the surface of the ground, such as creeks, streams, rivers, lakes, bays, and the ocean) and *Subsurface Waters* (that, is water found below the ground, primarily groundwater). Surface Waters are protected by the federal Clean Water Act as well as state law; Subsurface Waters are protected primarily by state law. The federal and state regulatory regimes are summarized below.

1-2.1.1. Federal Clean Water Act/NPDES

What is now known as the federal Clean Water Act, 33 U.S.C. §§ 1251 - 1387, was actually a set of amendments in 1972 to pre-existing federal statutes attempting to reduce water pollution primarily through state efforts. In perhaps the heady days of the burgeoning environmental movement, the CWA set ambitious goals:

> The objective of this chapter is to restore and maintain the chemical, physical, and biological integrity of the Nation's waters. In order to achieve this objective it is hereby declared that, consistent with the provisions of this chapter--
>
> **(1)** it is the national goal that the discharge of pollutants into the navigable waters be eliminated by 1985;
>
> **(2)** it is the national goal that wherever attainable, an interim goal of water quality which provides for the protection and propagation of fish, shellfish, and wildlife and provides for recreation in and on the water be achieved by July 1, 1983 . . . .

CWA § 101 (33 U.S.C. § 1251(a)). To achieve these goals, the CWA created a dramatically different, federal approach to the problem of water pollution.

The CWA regulates pollution in two ways. The first, and perhaps more well known, is through permits issued to dischargers that regulate the pollution those dischargers put into lakes, rivers, creeks, and streams. Consistent with the stated national goal of eliminating discharge of pollutants by 1985, the permits are called National Pollutant Discharge Elimination System (or NPDES) permits. The second method of regulation is through water quality standards that seek to force reductions in pollutant discharges through requirements that impose the standards via permits and through governing how discharge standards are set for permits. The perhaps best-known of these requirements are called Total Maximum Daily Loads, or TMDLs, that are discussed below.

What is important to understand is that the CWA utilizes an approach that has been called "cooperative federalism" which involves both federal and state regulators. The basic thrust of cooperative federalism is that the federal government (through the U.S. Environmental Protection Agency) sets minimum standards and then "delegates" the job of implementing those standards to states who agree to take on that regulatory job. EPA has delegated its CWA authority to DNREC. Thus, what DNREC does is use the federal standards (described below) to guide its regulation (empowered by the authority granted in Chapter 60 of Title 7 of the Delaware Code).

NPDES Permits

Under 33 U.S.C. § 1311 of the CWA, 33 U.S.C. § 1311, "the discharge of any pollutant by any person shall be unlawful" except in compliance with an NPDES permit. While that sounds quite broad, it is in fact more limited in scope because of the way the CWA defines "discharge of a pollutant." According to the definition section in the CWA, "discharge of a pollutant" "means (A) any addition of any pollutant to navigable waters from any point source, (B) any addition of any pollutant to the waters of the contiguous zone or the ocean from any point source other than a vessel or other floating craft." 33 U.S.C. § 1362(12). This means that there must be (1) an "addition" of a pollutant, (2) that the pollutant must be added to "navigable waters," and (3) that the addition must be coming from a "point source." Because the failure to have any of these three elements means that the prohibition of § 301 (and thus the CWA) does not apply, all three of these components have been litigated extensively. It is worth a brief comment on two of these elements.

First, the concept of "navigable waters" (also sometimes called "waters of the United States") is limited to waters that are connected to large-enough waters that a boat can navigate on them. You might not be able to float a boat on a small creek, but if that creek flows into a stream, which flows into a river, which flows to the Chesapeake Bay (on which a boat can surely navigate), then the creek is considered a "water of the United States" triggering CWA coverage because of its direct connection to the Bay. The flip side of this, however, is that some waters (think of an isolated pond in the middle of a field) might not have the requisite connection to trigger CWA coverage. As a result, not all water bodies are "navigable waters" under the CWA, and if a water body is not one, then § 301 (and thus the CWA) does not apply.

The other element worth discussing is the requirement that the pollution must come from a "point source." The CWA defines point source as

> any discernible, confined and discrete conveyance, including but not limited to any pipe, ditch, channel, tunnel, conduit, well, discrete fissure, container, rolling stock, concentrated animal feeding operation, or vessel or other floating craft, from which pollutants are or may be discharged. This term does not include agricultural stormwater discharges and return flows from irrigated agriculture.

33 U.S.C. § 1362(14). Thus, a factory with a pipe discharging into a stream is clearly a point source, and subject to NPDES permitting. Conversely, rainwater running off a field into that same stream is not coming from a point source, and therefore is not subject to NPDES permitting.[3] Thus, **not every source of pollution requires an NPDES permit.**

Assuming that the three elements of § 301 are present, the CWA requires that the point source obtain an NPDES permit (otherwise, it will be discharging pollutants in a manner which violates § 301). The NPDES program under the CWA requires the permitting authority (DNREC, thanks to its delegation from EPA) to impose limits on the discharge of pollutants by the permitted facility, as well as to impose various other requirements (like maintenance and reporting) that are designed to assure the facility is in compliance with its NPDES permit. One standard feature of all NPDES permits is that the permittee facility must regularly sample its discharge and report the results of that sampling to the permitting authority. These Discharge Monitoring Reports (or DMRs) become public records of the permitting authority (and thus subject to FOIA requests) and provide an easy record of when a facility has violated the discharge limits in the permit.

NPDES permits last for five years, and so must be renewed and reissued by the permitting authority. The process of applying for the initial permit and any renewal is subject to public notice, so it is possible to provide public comment and input on NPDES permitting decisions.

---

[3] Anything that does not meet the definition of a "point source" is called a "non-point source."

DNREC implements the NPDES program through regulations it has issued pursuant to its authority in Chapter 60 of Title 7 of the Delaware Code. The NPDES regulations can be found at 7 Del. Admin. C. 7201-6.0, which are part of DNREC's larger surface water regulatory program (available at http://regulations.delaware.gov/AdminCode/title7/7000/7200/7201.shtml#TopOfPage). These regulations specify what an NPDES permittee must do in order to obtain and comply with its NPDES permit.

One aspect of NPDES permitting also bears mention. Generally, point sources are unique enough that each requires its own NPDES permit tailored to its specific circumstances (both as to the wastewater it discharges as well as the receiving body into which it discharges). These tailored permits are called *individual NPDES permits*. Obtaining an individual NPDES permit requires a significant effort by the company. However, the CWA recognizes that some categories of dischargers are similar enough that the need for an NPDES permit can be satisfied by a permit that applies to any member of the category. These are called *general NPDES permits*, and the big difference is that dischargers seeking to proceed under a general permit do not need to file an individual application; instead, they need only file a Notice of Intent to proceed under the General Permit and, if DNREC agrees, simply comply with the General Permit's terms. There are general permits covering certain types of Concentrated Animal Feeding Operations (CAFOs) and stormwater discharges from certain construction sites.

Water Quality Standards

In addition to the regulation of point source discharges via the NPDES program, the CWA also seeks to reduce water pollution through what are known as Water Quality Standards (sometimes referred to as WQS). The Act envisions the WQS being developed by the states subject to federal review and approval. *See* CWA § 303 (33 U.S.C. § 1313).[4]

[4] The Act also envisions that, if a state has failed to create WQS, that the EPA can in fact promulgate WQS for use within the state. *See* CWA § 303(b) (33 U.S.C. § 1313(b)).

The Act envisions a process whereby the use for a particular water is designated by the state and then water quality criteria in the form of WQS are generated for that water based upon that designated use. Among the designated uses that are often recognized are drinking water sources, recreational uses (often designated as "fishable/swimmable"), secondary contact (meaning that, while one might not be swimming directly in the water, it is nevertheless safe so if one comes in contact with the water (for example, by water being splashed on you while in your canoe) you will not be harmed), as well as various agricultural and industrial uses. The WQS which then follow from that designation are designed to get the water quality to meet that designated use. Generally, the more contact that humans or wildlife would have with the water, the more protective a WQS needs to be in order to meet the designated use specified by the state.

WQS can take one of two forms. One form is called a "narrative" form, in which words are used to try to describe in general terms what the water quality criteria will be. The other form is known as a "numeric" standard. In these standards very specific numeric measurements of particular pollutants are identified as the standard for water quality.

The Act requires that each state identify those waters which are failing to obtain their designated uses because of some impairment by one or more pollutants and to rank, or prioritize, these "impaired waters." CWA § 303(d) (33 U.S.C. § 1313(d). This ranking is sometimes known as the "§ 303(d) list" of impaired waters. States are ultimately required to determine Total Maximum Daily Loads (TMDLs) of the impairing pollutant. Some people refer to TMDLs as a "pollution diet" because they restrict the amount of the pollutant that point and non-point sources can discharge into the receiving water so that the water quality will eventually improve and the designated use can be obtained. In a TMDL, each point source in the watershed is assigned a Wasteload Allocation (WLA) of the pollutant, which must then be incorporated into its NPDES permit.

DNREC has promulgated regulations governing WQS and has established 28 different TMDLs for Delaware waterbodies. These regulations and TMDLs can be found at 7 Del. Admin. C. § 7400, which is available at http://regulations.delaware.gov/AdminCode/title7/7000/7400/index.shtml.

1-2.1.2. *State-Specific Regulations*

In addition to regulation under the CWA, DNREC also regulates waters of the state of Delaware. These include:

- Discharges to surface waters of the state that are not subject to NPDES regulation. The regulations for this are available at 7 Del. Admin. C. 7201, http://regulations.delaware.gov/AdminCode/title7/7000/7200/7201.shtml#TopOfPage

- Discharges to subsurface waters of the state. Such discharges can occur from septic and on-site wastewater treatment disposal systems that seek to infiltrate the treated wastewater via such things as Rapid Infiltration Beds or Spray irrigation; the regulations for such discharges are available at 7 Del. Admin. C. 7101, http://regulations.delaware.gov/AdminCode/title7/7000/7100/7101.shtml#TopOfPage Such discharges can also occur from underground injection wells; the regulations for these sources are at 7 Del. Admin. C. 7102, available at http://regulations.delaware.gov/AdminCode/title7/7000/7100/7102.shtml#TopOfPage

- Water withdrawals and allocations are regulated at 7 Del. Admin. C. 7301 – 7303, available at http://regulations.delaware.gov/AdminCode/title7/7000/7300/index.shtml

Wetlands are also water resources subject to regulation. If the wetlands are connected to waters of the United States, activities in those wetlands are governed by federal law pursuant to Section 404 of the CWA, 33 U.S.C. § 1344. The U.S. Army Corps of Engineers plays a central role in federal regulation of wetlands. Delaware has passed a separate law, The Wetlands Act, found at Chapter 66 of Title 7 in the Delaware Code. The Wetlands Act defines "wetlands" as

> those lands above the mean low water elevation including any bank, marsh, swamp, meadow, flat or other low land subject to tidal action in the State along the Delaware Bay and Delaware River, Indian River Bay, Rehoboth Bay, Little and Big Assawoman Bays, the coastal

> inland waterways, or along any inlet, estuary or tributary waterway or any portion thereof, including those areas which are now or in this century have been connected to tidal waters, whose surface is at or below an elevation of 2 feet above local mean high water, and upon which may grow or is capable of growing any but not necessarily all [a list specific plants].

7 Del. C. § 6603(h). It is worth noting that only land "subject to tidal action" are wetlands under the Act; if there is no tidal action, the land is not a "wetland" even though it may be wet and have some of the plants listed in the definition. The Act then requires a permit from DNREC for any activity within a wetland. The regulations governing activity in wetlands are at 7 Del. Admin. C. 7502, available at
http://regulations.delaware.gov/AdminCode/title7/7000/7500/7502.shtml#TopOfPage

Finally, "subaqueous lands" (defined as "submerged lands and tidelands," *see* 7 Del. C. § 7202(g)) are governed by the Subaqueous Lands Act, 7 Del. C. § 7201 *et seq*. Docks and marinas can involve subaqueous lands, and are regulated by 7 Del. Admin. C. 7501, available at
http://regulations.delaware.gov/AdminCode/title7/7000/7500/7501.shtml#TopOfPage
In addition, because the State is considered to own certain subaqueous lands in public trust, other uses of these lands trigger regulation by 7 Del. Admin. C. 7504, available at
http://regulations.delaware.gov/AdminCode/title7/7000/7500/7504.shtml#TopOfPage

Not surprisingly, sometimes multiple sets of regulations may apply to a particular situation. For example, a person seeking to build a marina might trigger application of 7 Del. Admin. C. 7501 (governing the marina itself), 7504 (because the state must approve the use of public subaqueous lands), and even 7502 (to the extent the marina involves activity in wetlands).

1-2.2. Air Resources

DNREC's regulatory power over air resources derives from 7 Del. C. § 6003(a)(1), which prohibits persons from undertaking "any activity . . . In a way which may cause or contribute to discharge of an air contaminant. Regulation and control of air pollution has a federal regulatory component derived from the Clean Air Act, 42 U.S.C. §§ 7401 – 7671q, and state-specific regulations as well.

1-2.2.1 Clean Air Act

The Clean Air Act, 42 U.S.C. §§ 7401 – 7671q ("CAA"), became law in 1970, one year after NEPA and two years before the amendments that became the CWA. The CAA creates a federal system that recognizes and relies upon the States to help implement the federal standards. One of the CAA's goals is to "protect and enhance the quality of the Nation's air resources so as to promote the public health and welfare and the productive capacity of its population." CAA § 101(b)(1) (42 U.S.C. § 7401(b)(1)). To achieve that goal, the CAA covers a wide range of sources (both stationary and mobile), problems (air quality, acid rain, regional haze, and stratospheric ozone, to name a few), and solutions. The resulting regulatory system is very complex, relying on national standards for some pollutants and layers of differing regulation of sources.

One way to approach the CAA is to think of it as promulgating a series of national minimum standards that are to be implemented by the States with oversight by the EPA. The first of these are the National Ambient Air Quality Standards, or NAAQS. EPA has identified 6 criteria pollutants for which it has developed NAAQS: sulfur oxides (often designated as SOx), ozone, particulate matter (PM) (first as PM-10, then as PM-2.5, where the number indicates the minimum size in microns of the particle at which the regulation begins), nitrogen oxides (often designated as NOx), lead, and carbon monoxide (CO). Once standards for each criteria pollutant are set, each state must then develop a State Implementation Plan (SIP) for how it will achieve the NAAQS. How much needs to be done depends on whether the State is "in attainment" (that is, its air quality meets or "attains" the NAAQS) or in nonattainment. SIPs for States in attainment must have a plan to maintain attainment via regulations called Prevention of Significant Deterioration (PSD), while SIPs for States in nonattainment must implement regulations that ratchet down the pollution via regulations requiring the use of Reasonably Achievable Control Technologies (RACT) and New Source Review (NSR). Needless to say, these regulatory regimes are very complex.

A second set of federal standards seek to regulate certain types of air pollution sources. These are called National Source Performance Standards (NSPS), which basically limit the amounts of pollution each type of source can emit.

The third major type of federal standards relate to Hazardous Air Pollutants (HAPs), which are regulated through National Emission Standards for Hazardous Air Pollutants (NESHAPs). These standards impose limits on the amount of HAPs that can be emitted, and therefore impose some technology requirements on major sources.

Title V of the CAA attempts to bring PSD, NSR, NSPS, and NESHAPs together into a single, "Title V Permit" for emitting facilities. It is in this permitting process that many issues concerning these regulatory schemes are worked out. For example, PSD, NSR, NSPS, and NESHAPs apply to "major" sources of pollutants (generally defined as the potential to emit a certain quantity of the pollutant), and so some emitters will seek to be a "minor" source, either because the facility could simply never emit the minimum quantity to be a major source (these are called *natural* minor sources) or by agreeing to limit emissions through operational controls to levels below the major source threshold (these are called *synthetic* minor sources). Title V permits generally require sources to keep and submit records of their compliance with all limits (like the DMRs under the CWA), which can provide a roadmap for determining a facility's CAA compliance.

The CAA utilizes the same concept of "cooperative federalism" as the Clean Water Act: the federal government sets standards then delegates the regulation and enforcement to the states. DNREC implements the CAA in Delaware through its Division of Air Quality. Over 50 sets of regulations, found at 7 Del. Admin. C. 1101 – 1150, govern DNREC's regulation of air pollution, available at http://regulations.delaware.gov/AdminCode/title7/1000/1100/index.shtml

1-2.3. Coastal Zone

The Coastal Zone Act, 7 Del. C. § 7001 *et seq.* ("CZA"), is an environmental regulation unique to Delaware. At its core, it prohibits new "heavy industry" and "bulk product transfer facilities," and requires permits for new "manufacturing facilities," within the Coastal Zone (a defined area running along the eastern coast of Delaware). 7 Del. C. § 7003, 7004. "New" means anything commenced after June 28, 1971 (the day the CZA was passed); thus, heavy industry operations and bulk product transfer facilities that were operating on June 28, 1971 and operate today are allowed to continue to operate as "nonconforming uses" (and can even "expand"/"extend" their operation via permit). Permits (whether for new manufacturing uses or expansions/extensions of nonconforming uses) must be considered under six different factors that include environmental and economic impacts. 7 Del. C. § 7004(b).[5]

DNREC enforces and administers the CZA. 7 Del. C. § 7005. It performs two roles that allow for citizen participation. The first involves "status decisions." A person or entity contemplating engaging in activity in the Coastal Zone can request that the Secretary determine the status of the proposed activity under the CZA. The person/entity submits a "Request for Status Decision," and once it is complete, the Secretary publishes the request and solicits public comment in a tight, 10-day window. After the comment period closes, the Secretary must decide within 15 days whether: the proposed activity is prohibited under the CZA, is allowed under the CZA but requires a permit, or that the activity is not regulated under the CZA. The purpose of the status decision is to allow a potential operator to find out the project's status under the CZA without going through a full application process.

---

[5] These factors are: environmental impact (which includes probable air and water pollution; likely destruction of wetlands, flora and fauna; impacts on drainage, erosion, and flood control; effects on surface and subsurface water resources; and the "likelihood of generation of glare, heat, noise, vibration, radiation, electromagnetic interference and obnoxious odors"), economic effect, aesthetic effect, effects on neighboring land uses, and compliance with local zoning and comprehensive plans.

The other opportunity for public participation arises when DNREC considers an application for a CZA permit. Public comment and a public hearing may occur in connection with each permit application.

In 2017, the General Assembly amended the CZA to allow 14 nonconforming use sites (13 of which are in New Castle County, one in Kent County) to seek a "conversion permit" that would allow site owner to build a new heavy industry use or bulk product transfer facility that might have otherwise been prohibited under the old version of the Act. *See* 7 Del. C. § 7014. There are numerous statutory requirements that must be met to get a conversion permit. Regulations for conversion permits are, as of the writing of this Guide, being finalized.

1-3. Areas In Which DNREC Does Not Have Authority

While DNREC has significant regulatory authority, there are certain areas that have direct or indirect effects on the environment that DNREC cannot and does not regulate. Two important areas are worth mentioning here.

1-3.1 NEPA

The National Environmental Policy Act (NEPA), 42 U.S.C. §§ 4321 – 4370h, was the first modern federal environmental statute. It includes lofty language, stating that one of its purposes is to "[t]o declare a national policy which will encourage productive and enjoyable harmony between man and his environment; to promote efforts which will prevent or eliminate damage to the environment and biosphere and stimulate the health and welfare of man . . . ." 42 U.S.C. § 4321. Its straightforward requirements concerning the assessment of environmental impacts are deceptively simple: when the requirements for a NEPA analysis are triggered, federal agencies are required to examine environmental impacts. In practice, NEPA is more modest in scope.

NEPA requires that, "in every recommendation or report on proposals for legislation and other major Federal actions significantly affecting the quality of the human environment," a "detailed statement" that analyzes (among other things) the environmental impacts of the proposed action, including adverse environmental impacts that cannot be avoided if the proposal is implemented, and alternatives to the proposed activity. 42 U.S.C. § 4322(C). This language imposes several requirements, each of which are potential ways to limit the NEPA analysis: the action must be "federal" (i.e., NEPA does not apply to state actions); it must be "major" (so that minor actions do not trigger the full scope of NEPA); it must "significantly affect" (so actions that minimally affect do not trigger the full scope of NEPA); and the effect must be on "the quality of the human environment." Each of these phrases has been litigated extensively.

There are two tools of NEPA analysis: the Environmental Assessment (EA) and the Environmental Impact Statement (EIS). The EA is, by design, more limited in nature and scope than the EIS. In some respects, an EA is conducted to determine whether or not more examination of environmental impacts is needed. An EA will lead to one of two conclusions: either (1) a finding that there is no significant environmental impact requiring further analysis (called a "FONSI"- which stands for "Finding Of No Significant Impact") which ends the agency's environmental impact analysis; or (2) the need to conduct the more intensive review of an Environmental Impact Statement ("EIS"). There are general federal regulations governing the NEPA process. *See* 40 C.F.R. Parts 1501 – 1508. Each federal agency establishes its own regulations governing how it will conduct NEPA processes that are designed to add additional, agency-specific detail to the general regulations.

Because an EIS requires a significant amount of work and can tend to slow down agency decision making, it can sometime appear that agencies want to avoid going down that route whenever possible. All agencies have what are called "categorical exclusions"—categories of activities that the agency claims do not generate an environmental impact and so need to impact analysis. If something is not categorically excluded, the EA process quite often leads to a FONSI—again, cutting off the need for further analysis in an EIS. What this means is that **NEPA does not always require an Environmental Impact Statement be prepared**. A federal agency may be able to show that an EIS need not be done because of a categorical exclusion or because the EA led to a FONSI.

As noted earlier, NEPA only applies to federal actors—generally federal agencies, but can also cover persons acting on behalf of the federal government. This means, of course, that **NEPA does not regulate state agencies or officials. As a result, DNREC (or any other Delaware agency) is not required to engage in NEPA processes.**[6]

A third aspect of NEPA is that it does not mandate particular decisions. In other words, **NEPA does not require the federal government to undertake the most environmentally friendly or beneficial course of action**. Instead, it simply requires the government to identify the environmental impacts of a decision so that federal officials will make a fully-informed decision. The fully-informed official may choose a more environmentally detrimental option than other options considered and not violate NEPA. Thus, NEPA is more about making sure that the official is fully-informed; if some environmental impact should have been but was not analyzed (what courts sometimes call a "hard look"), then the official is not fully-informed, and the decision would violate NEPA. As a result, the vast majority of NEPA challenges are about the failure to consider adequately some environmental impact that should have been considered. In this sense, NEPA is more about the *procedure* than the *substance* of a federal decision.

1-3.2. Zoning

DNREC does not have the authority to engage in regulation that traditionally falls within the area of zoning. In *Sussex County v. DNREC*,[7] Sussex County challenged a DNREC regulation called the Pollution Control Strategy for the Inland Bays ("PCS"). The PCS imposed 100–foot buffers (that is, areas in which development could not take place) around water bodies (streams, creeks, lakes, etc.) connected to the Inland Bays so that the buffers could absorb nutrient pollutants like nitrogen and phosphorus and thereby prevent those pollutants from entering the Inland Bays watershed. The Superior Court and the Supreme Court

---

[6] This does not mean that NEPA never surfaces in activity within Delaware; if a federal agency is involved, NEPA applies to the actions of that federal agency. So, for example, federal funds being loaned or granted for a project in Delaware might trigger NEPA for the federal agency giving the funds. Even in that situation, however, NEPA does not apply to the state agencies involved; only the federal agency must comply with NEPA.

[7] 34 A.3d 1087 (Del. 2011).

both found that DNREC, by imposing buffers, was engaged in the regulation of land use that is the essence of zoning—a governmental power reserved to the counties in the state. Because DNREC had no power to engage in zoning, the buffer requirement was improper, and therefore struck down. As a result, zoning issues must be fought at the county level.[8]

[8] The rules governing zoning are beyond the scope of this Guide.

CHAPTER 2
OPPORTUNITIES FOR PUBLIC PARTICIPATION IN DELAWARE'S ENVIRONMENTAL REGULATORY SCHEME

Delaware's Environmental Regulatory Structure creates different opportunities for members of the public to weigh in on regulatory decisions. These opportunities can be divided into those arising *before* the final decision is made ("Pre-Decision Opportunities") and those arising *after* the decision is made ("Post-Decision Opportunities").

2-1. Pre-Decision Opportunities for Public Participation

Most environmental laws require that a person seeking to engage in a regulated activity obtain a permit or other permission from DNREC to do so.[9] To seek such permission, the person must file an application or request with DNREC. When such a request is made, DNREC will generally provide public notice that the application has been received. Chapter 60 requires that:

> upon receipt of an application in proper form, the Secretary shall advertise in a newspaper of general circulation in the county in which the activity is

---

[9] For example, 7 Del. C. § 6003(a) provides:

> (a) No person shall, without first having obtained a permit from the Secretary, undertake any activity:
>
> (1) In a way which may cause or contribute to the discharge of an air contaminant; or
>
> (2) In a way which may cause or contribute to discharge of a pollutant into any surface or ground water; or
>
> (3) In a way which may cause or contribute to withdrawal of ground water or surface water or both; or
>
> (4) In a way which may cause or contribute to the collection, transportation, storage, processing or disposal of solid wastes, regardless of the geographic origin or source of such solid wastes; or
>
> (5) To construct, maintain or operate a pipeline system including any appurtenances such as a storage tank or pump station; or
>
> (6) To construct any water facility; or
>
> (7) To plan or construct any highway corridor which may cause or contribute to the discharge of an air contaminant or discharge of pollutants into any surface or ground water.

proposed and in a daily newspaper of general circulation throughout the State:

(1) The fact that the application has been received;

(2) A brief description of the nature of the application; and

(3) The place at which a copy of the application may be inspected.

7 Del. C. § 6004(b). This public notice will often specify a limited time period in which public comments and requests for public hearings will be received by DNREC.

2-1.1 Public Comment

Once the public notice indicates that public comments can be submitted, you can submit written comments to DNREC. Suggestions on how to draft such comments are contained in Part II of this Guide. The comments need to be in writing and submitted by the deadline specified in the public notice. All timely written comments submitted to DNREC become part of the record before the Secretary.

2-1.2 Public Hearings

As noted above, the public notice of an application will often include language about public hearings. There are two ways in which a decision to hold a public hearing can be triggered. The first is that DNREC decides on its own that a public hearing should be held. 7 Del. C. § 6004(b) describes this approach as follows: "A public hearing may be held on any application if the Secretary deems it to be in the best interest of the State to do so." Historically, the Secretary has used this approach to simply go ahead and set a public hearing when the permit or activity is controversial or for which a large amount of public interest (often measured by the volume of public comments) exists. The Secretary will provide public notice of a public hearing set under this approach.

The second way a public hearing can be set is when one or more members of the public request that a hearing be held. 7 Del. C. § 6004(b) describes this approach as follows: "The Secretary shall hold a public hearing on an application, if he or she receives a meritorious request for a hearing within a reasonable time as stated in the advertisement." Two things are worth noting here. First, a request is considered "meritorious" if "it exhibits a familiarity with the application and a reasoned statement of the permit's probable impact." *Id.* In other words, the request needs to say more than simply that one wants a hearing; it needs to explain in some detail *why* a hearing should be held. Second, the "reasonable time" within which to make a request is defined as 15 days, unless the public notice says otherwise. Thus, there is a time limit for making a request. Assuming the request is timely and meritorious, DNREC will usually set and hold a public hearing.

Most public hearings on permit applications follow a similar format. A court reporter takes down everything that is said at the hearing once the presiding Hearing Officer calls the hearing to order. The applicant makes a presentation about what it intends to do. DNREC then provides certain information (usually, proof of what it has done—a copy of the application, proof of publication of the public notices, etc. are made exhibits. The Hearing Officer presiding over the hearing then allows for public comment to be made by anyone attending the meeting. Comments can be submitted in writing, or an attendee can step up to the microphone and say what he or she wants to say about the permit. Often, the Hearing Officer imposes time limits on each commenter. Once all oral comments are made, the hearing is closed, and with it the record as well—meaning that no more public comment can be made (unless someone asks, and the Hearing Officer grants, an extension of time for submission of public comments). Once that comment period closes, the public will have no more chances to comment until the Secretary issues a decision on the application.

The transcript of the hearing, as well as all exhibits and written comments submitted at the hearing, become part of the record before the Secretary.[10]

[10] Comments submitted to the Hearing Officer outside the public hearing pursuant to the instructions and by the deadline provided in the Public Notice also become part of the record before the Secretary.

Once the public hearing is completed and the public comment period closed, the Hearing Officer then has to make a recommendation to the Secretary about whether the permit should be issued or action taken. It is common practice for the Hearing Officer to ask relevant DNREC staff to prepare a response to the issues raised at the public hearing. This response gets formalized into a Technical Response Memorandum ("TRM") which staff then gives to the Hearing Officer. The Hearing Officer creates a Hearing Officer's Report which summarizes the evidence and public comment and creates a recommendation for the Secretary. The TRM will be attached to the Hearing Officer's Report.

Occasionally, DNREC staff might reach out to the permit applicant (or the applicant to DNREC staff) after the public hearing/public comment closes in order to address issues or concerns raised during the hearing/comment process. These interactions might affect the TRM or other action staff takes.

What is important to realize is that this post-hearing/comment process (the TRM, applicant-staff interactions) takes place outside public view without any opportunity for the public to comment on or participate in this process. This is important because, while the TRM and perhaps some of the applicant staff-interactions end up in the record before the Secretary, the public has no opportunity to supplement the record in light of the changes and further analysis happening in the post-hearing/comment period.

2-2. Post-Decision Opportunities for Public Participation

Once the final decision is made, it is usually set forth in a written Secretary's Order. The Secretary usually writes an Order that incorporates the Hearing Officer's Report (and therefore any TRM attached to it) and sets forth the Secretary's reasoning for his/her decision. The Secretary's Order serves as the embodiment of the final decision.

At this point in the process, the opportunities for public participation are limited to appeals of the Secretary's decision.

Delaware law contemplates that appeals of Secretary's Orders go through as many as 3 stages of appellate review. The first is administrative in nature; the party seeking to appeal must first file an appeal with a designated administrative appeals board. A decision by the designated board can then be appealed to the Superior Court, and decisions by the Superior Court can then be appealed to the Delaware Supreme Court.

2-2.1 Administrative Board Appeals

Delaware law has created two administrative appeals board to review decisions of the DNREC Secretary. With the exception of appeals under the Coastal Zone Act, all appeals of Secretary decisions go to the Environmental Appeals Board; appeals under the CZA go to the Coastal Zone Industrial Control Board.

2-2.1.1 Appeals to the Environmental Appeals Board

The Environmental Appeals Board (EAB) was established with the passage of Chapter 60 of Title 7. Section 6007 creates the EAB. It consists of 7 Delaware residents, appointed by the Governor and confirmed by the Senate, who serve three-year terms (although the Chair "serves at the Governor's pleasure," and so could presumably be removed at any time). The statute requires that each county have at least 2 members, and that there be political balance (based on party membership). 7 Del. C. § 6007(a).

The EAB is a "quasi-judicial review board." 7 Del. C. § 6007(b). In practice, this means that the Board acts like a court, but without the all of the restrictions (like rules of evidence) that a court might impose. The Board has adopted regulations which govern practice before it,[11] and § 5.4 specifically states "Strict rules of evidence shall not apply. All evidence having probative value commonly accepted by a reasonably prudent person in the conduct of his or her affairs shall be admitted."

---

[11] You can find these regulations at https://regulations.delaware.gov/AdminCode/title7/100/105.shtml.

The EAB has the power to affirm, modify, or reverse the Secretary's decision. In acting, the EAB is subject to the requirements of the Delaware Administrative Procedures Act, 29 Del. C. § 10101 *et seq*.

Appeals to the EAB must be filed with the Board "within 20 days after receipt of the Secretary's decision or publication of the decision." 7 Del. C. § 6008(a). The "or" in this statutory language suggests that the later of the two events controls (in other words, if publication happens after receipt, then the period runs from the publication date). The "publication" referenced in the statute refers to public notice that is published in newspapers in the State. Every Wednesday and Sunday, DNREC publishes public notice of its actions in state newspapers; the 20 days from publication would run from that date. The safest course of action (when possible) is to calculate the 20 days from the date of the Secretary's Order itself, so that the question of "receipt" and "publication" are rendered irrelevant to the question of whether an appeal is timely.

Appeals to the EAB are limited to "[a]ny person whose interest is substantially affected by any action of the Secretary." 7 Del. C. § 6008(a). The notion of being "substantially affected" raises the issue of standing (discussed more fully in Part II of this Guide). In short, a citizen must have standing in order to have an appeal heard by the EAB.

Appeals to the EAB commence with the filing of a Statement of Appeal. The EAB's regulations list the required contents:

> 2.1 The request for an appeal shall be submitted in the form of a written statement. The statement shall set forth clearly and concisely the following:
>
> > 2.1.1 the interest which has been substantially affected;
> >
> > 2.1.2 an allegation that the decision is improper; and
> >
> > 2.1.3 the reasons why the decision is improper.

The request for appeal should be stated with sufficient specificity to notify the Board and [DNREC] of the reasons for the appeal.

2.2 The written statement shall also set forth an estimate of the number of witnesses and the time involved in presenting the appeal at the public hearing.

The EAB also requires payment of a $50 filing fee to commence an appeal. These regulatory requirements mean that the Statement of Appeal must include detail and list all of the issues the appellant would raise in a hearing before the Board. The failure to list a reason why the decision is wrong may mean that the appellant will not be able to raise that issue at the hearing. As a result, the Statement of Appeal requires thought and planning to make sure it is complete.

The statute requires that the EAB conduct a public hearing on every appeal, 7 Del. C. § 6008(a). At least 20 days before the hearing, the Board must issue public notice of hearing specifying when and where it will take place. To prepare for the hearing, the EAB regulations require that, at least 20 days before the hearing date, the parties (the appellant, DNREC, and any other parties that have sought to intervene in the appeal—usually the permittee if the appeal is about the issuance of a permit) must conduct a Pre-Hearing Conference. Ten days before the Pre-Hearing Conference, the parties must exchange lists of their exhibits and witnesses so that everyone knows what everyone else intends to offer at the hearing. Having exchanged those witness and exhibit lists, the Pre-Hearing Conference then does the following:

The purpose of the conference is to:

3.1.1 Determine the extent to which the appellant and the Department may agree about facts in the appeal;

3.1.2 Identify the witnesses each party will call at the hearing and to receive a brief summary of the testimony the witnesses will present;

3.1.3 Identify all documents which the parties intend to introduce at the hearing;

3.1.4 Resolve any and all procedural matters;

3.1.5 Generally inform the Board and the parties about the substance of the hearing; and

3.1.6 Identify issues.

3.2 No fewer than ten (10) days prior to the date set for the pre-hearing conference, [DNREC] and the appellant shall submit to the Board's attorney and to each other, a list of the witnesses they intend to call at the hearing and a list of the documents, including relevant portions of those documents, and other evidence which they intend to submit into evidence at the hearing. These lists shall be finalized at the pre-hearing conference.

3.3 The parties shall submit final witness and document lists and shall raise all objections to such witnesses and documents at the pre-hearing conference.

The failure to identify witnesses or exhibits during this process may result in the Board refusing to allow them at the hearing.

The parties to the appeal will need to submit copies of their exhibits to the Board (usually 10 copies) and to each party before the hearing so that everyone has the exhibits that will be used at the hearing.

The public hearing itself is held before the Board. Appellant goes first, presenting its evidence and witnesses. DNREC, any other party to the appeal, and the individual members of the Board all get to ask questions of any witness testifying. After the appellant's case is complete, third parties get to present, and then DNREC goes last. Once all of the parties are done presenting witnesses and evidence, the Board may hear closing arguments and then will go into executive session to reach its decision. It usually announces its decision in the form of a vote taken in public.

Once the Board has reached a decision, it must set forth its decision in a written order that complies with the Administrative Procedures Act. The Board has 90 days from the date of its vote to issue its written decision. The written decision can then be the subject of an appeal to the Superior Court.

2-2.1.2 Appeals to the Coastal Zone Industrial Control Board

The Coastal Zone Industrial Control Board ("CZICB") exists solely to handle appeals of the Secretary's decisions under the Coastal Zone Act. Created by 7 Del. C. § 7006, the CZICB differs from the EAB in that several of 9 members are designated by the statute via governmental positions they hold. The State's Director of the Division of Small Business, as well as the chairpersons of the New Castle County, Kent County, and Sussex County Planning Commissions are members, with the other 5 positions filled via appointment by the Governor and confirmation by the Senate. There are geographic and political limitations on the membership.

The CZICB serves two statutorily-specified roles. The first is to approve any regulations under the Coastal Zone Act issued by DNREC. 7 Del. C. § 7005(b). The second is to hear appeals of decisions by the Secretary under the Act. 7 Del. C. § 7007(a). The Act requires the Board to hold a public hearing on any appeal filed with the Board.

Appeals to the CZICB are initiated by filing a Notice of Appeal with the Board. While there are no specific regulations governing what needs to be in the Notice of Appeal, in general the Notice should be specific in stating the grounds for appeal, as the Notice may limit what the appellant can raise during the public hearing. Appeals can only be brought by "[a]ny person aggrieved by a final decision of the Secretary of the Department of Natural Resources and Environmental Control under § 7005(a) or § 7014 of this title." Delaware courts have interpreted the "person aggrieved" language of the Act as basically the same as the "person substantially affected" language governing appeals to the EAB, and this triggers the issue of standing.

The Act imposes much tighter timeframes on appeals to the CZICB than those imposed on appeal to the EAB. The appeal itself must be filed within 14 days "following announcement by the Secretary of the Department of Natural Resources and Environmental Control of his or her decision." 7 Del. C. § 7007(b). The CZICB "must hold a hearing and render its decision in the form of a final order within 60 days following receipt of the appeal notification." *Id.* Given that the CZICB must give public notice of the hearing at least 20 days before the hearing date, the window for holding the hearing is quite small.

The Act grants the CZICB the following powers:

> The Board may affirm or reverse the decision of the Secretary of the Department of Natural Resources and Environmental Control with respect to applicability of any provisions of this chapter to a proposed use; it may modify any permit granted by the Secretary of the Department of Natural Resources and Environmental Control, grant a permit denied by the Secretary, deny a permit or confirm the Secretary's grant of a permit. Provided, however, that the Board may grant no permit for uses prohibited in § 7003 of this title.

7 Del. C. § 7007(a). The first sentence grants the Board review authority over status decisions, while the latter sentences grant authority over permit decisions.

The hearing process before the CZICB is similar to that before the EAB, but there are two differences. First, unlike the EAB, which can deliberate in executive session, the CZICB deliberates in open session so the public can hear the deliberations (although the deliberations are not recorded in the transcript of the hearing). Second, the CZICB will take public comment at the end of the hearing (often, after it has already announced its decision).

2-2.2 Appeals to the Superior Court

Decisions of the EAB and CZICB can be appealed to the Superior Court. Such appeals must be filed within 30 days of the issuance of the written decision. Appeals require the filing of a Notice of Appeal and the paying of a filing fee, usually in excess of $200. The Notice of Appeal must be served on all parties in the underlying Board action (and the Sheriff charges $30 each party to serve the Notice).

The appeal generally involves the filing of briefs with the Court setting forth the arguments concerning whether the Board's decision was correct. There are court rules governing the briefs, for everything from font size to page limits.

Generally, the Court's review is limited to whether the Board's factual findings are supported by "substantial evidence" in the record, and whether the Board's legal conclusions are contrary to law.

2-2.3 Appeals to the Supreme Court

Decisions of the Superior Court can be appealed to the Delaware Supreme Court. Such appeals must be filed within 30 days of the Superior Court's decision, and are subject to fees and rules governing briefing. The focus of these appeals is solely on whether the Superior Court acted properly in its ruling.

CHAPTER 3
EFFECTIVE ADVOCACY DURING THE PERMIT ISSUANCE PROCESS

A large part of environmental regulation happens via DNREC-issued permits. In issuing a permit, DNREC must consider and apply the relevant law and regulations to determine whether the applicant should be issued or denied the requested permit. Concerned citizens want DNREC to apply the law correctly in the permit process and should let DNREC know if it is not doing so. Thus, it makes sense to focus on how to advocate effectively in the permit process itself.

For citizens who are not the permit applicant, the primary vehicle for advocacy in the permit process is public comment. This Chapter provides guidance on how to develop and make effective public comments in the permit process.

3-1. Preparing To Make Public Comments

Effective public comment involves preparation before a word of comment is made—in other words, doing your homework can make your public comment more effective and impactful. This preparation involves developing the knowledge necessary to comment and a strategy for how to comment.

3-1.1 Know What's Coming

The first aspect of knowledge is knowing that a particular permit is being considered by DNREC. While some projects may be known in the community, the details about permits being considered by DNREC might not.

Fortunately, most state environmental statutes or regulations require that DNREC give public notice when the permit application process commences or is ongoing. Chapter 60 of Title 7—which controls many of the bigger regulatory programs of DNREC, specifically requires that, with a few exceptions (*see* 7 Del. C. § 6004(c)):

> upon receipt of an application in proper form, the Secretary shall advertise in a newspaper of general circulation in the county in which the activity is

proposed and in a daily newspaper of general circulation throughout the State:

(1) The fact that the application has been received;

(2) A brief description of the nature of the application; and

(3) The place at which a copy of the application may be inspected.

7 Del. C. § 6004(b). Similar notice requirements are in other Delaware statutes. *See e.g.*, 7 Del. C. § 6608(b) (Wetlands Act); 7 Del. C. § 7207(d) (Subaqueous Lands Act). Note that the required notice includes not just the fact that an application has been received, but also a description of what is being proposed and where you can go to review the actual application.

The notice must be published in newspapers—those small print Legal Notices you might see in your paper. Reading through them can strain your eyes. A simpler was to get the same notice is to look at the DNREC website, which posts all public notices issued by the agency. *See* https://dnrec.alpha.delaware.gov/public-notices/. You can also sign up to receive emails of DNREC public notices by subscribing at https://dnrec.alpha.delaware.gov/subscribe/. You might receive more notices than just about the project you are interested in, but a subscription can make sure you don't miss out.

Checklist 3.1 at the end of this Chapter can be a good guide for gathering the information you need for the public comment process—especially the deadlines and methods by which you must submit your comments.

3-1.2 Become Knowledgeable About A Project

Once you know that there is a permit of interest, the real work now begins. Effective comments require you to know the details of the project, so you need to gather as much information as you can. Your best source of information—at least initially—is the permit application itself. As noted above, DNREC's public notice will inform you "the place at which a copy of the application may be inspected." Historically, that meant you had to go to a DNREC office to look at a physical copy of the application, and sometimes you still must, but DNREC often puts application material on its website so that you can view it on your computer. Your first step should be to review the application to glean as much knowledge as you can. Although applications can be long and filled with technical information, there are some initial things you should be able to figure out from your review:

- Who is the applicant (that is, the person who is applying for the permit)?

- What type of permit is the applicant seeking? This will help you identify what law or regulations DNREC will use to consider the permit.

- What is the activity that the applicant plans to carry out with the permit?

- Where will the permitted activity take place?

All this initial information will give you a general understanding of what the permit would allow to happen. That information might allow you to decide whether the project is something about which you want or need to comment. For example, after reading the application you might decide that the permitted activity is small or insignificant enough that its impact will be limited. Or perhaps it is an activity which you view as positive. If so, you might decide that you don't need to submit public comment. That's a perfectly fine decision to make—provided you make it with sufficient knowledge.

If you are not sure about the need to comment, or are sure you definitely do want to comment because your initial application review suggests the project is big enough or will have impacts you are concerned about, then you need to dig deeper. Your focus should be on two different areas:

1. Legal: What is the law and regulations that will govern the permit request?

2. Factual: How does the permit application stack up against the governing law?

The Legal aspect here is important because it defines the terms of what DNREC will use when assessing the application. Generally, what DNREC does when reviewing a permit application is figure out what the governing regulations require and then assess whether those regulatory requirements have been satisfied.

For example, the current regulations governing wastewater treatment systems that dispose of treated wastewater by spraying it on a field to irrigate crops (something called "spray irrigation") requires that a Hydrologic Suitability Report (HSR) be prepared to show that the spray irrigation fields can in fact handle the water that will be sprayed upon them. The regulations require specific analyses that must be in an HSR. DNREC will review an application to see if it has an HSR and whether that HSR both has all the required analyses and that the analyses show the field is suitable for spray irrigation. Thus, knowledge that the regulations require an HSR can help you reviewing the application because you will know to look for the HSR and then whether the HSR meets those regulatory requirements. An effective public comment is one that can show DNREC what a legal requirement is (the applicant must submit an HSR) and then how the applicant has not satisfied the requirement (no HSR was submitted or the HSR does not contain their required elements or make the required showings).

Determining the governing law is not always easy. Sometimes, the application will give you some idea because the applicant will be trying to show DNREC that it has complied with the applicable regulations. You can then look up the regulations using the links and tools identified in Part I of this Guide. Even when you find the regulations, they are not always easy to understand. The Clinic may be able to help you get a general understanding of what the regulations require, or you can simply rely upon your own ability to figure it out. The goal is to use the legal requirements to help frame your comments.

Armed with a general understanding of what the law requires, you can now review the application to see how it stacks up against those regulations. Are there required things that were missed? Does the application provide information that is inconsistent with what the regulations require? Those are the types of points that make effective public comments because they go to the core of DNREC's job: applying the law correctly to a given situation.

A second source of information can be Freedom of Information Act (FOIA) requests. The state FOIA statute, at 29 Del. C. § 10001, gives citizens the right to request and obtain public records from state agencies. Typically, you don't need to FOIA information about the permit application itself (because DNREC makes the application available for public inspection), but sometimes—when digging deeper into an applicant or other related projects—you might want information beyond the application itself. While FOIA is its own set of issues that may be worthy of its own Citizen Guide, three general principles should govern your use of FOIA:

- FOIA the right governmental agency. Governmental agencies only control the information they have; DNREC, for example, cannot get information in the files of Sussex County. So you need to make sure you ask for the information from the agency which has it. If you are not sure which agency has it, you may need to submit FOIA requests to each agency.

- Comply with the agency's FOIA's procedures. There is no one standard FOIA procedure across all governmental units in Delaware. As a result, you need to make sure that you follow the procedure used by the agency to which you are submitting your FOIA request. DNREC has a specific link on its webpage that allows you to submit a FOIA request for DNREC records directly online, but not all state agencies do.

- Recognize that certain types of records can be withheld from production because of exceptions under the FOIA statute. For example, a personnel record of a government employee is not available under FOIA. As a result, you may not be able to get all the documents you want.

- FOIA takes time and money. Governmental agencies have time to respond to a FOIA request, and the ability to get extensions under certain circumstances. Governmental agencies also can charge you for time to pull records and for copies of the records; some agencies are more aggressive than others when it comes to those rules. You need to factor in the time and money aspects when using FOIA to obtain information for public comments.

Lastly, you might be able to obtain information from public sources. The Internet opens vast amounts of information for review. While you can obtain valuable background information that can augment what your review of the application reveals, you need to be careful of two things: (1) Not everything on the Internet is accurate; and (2) internet searching can be a "rabbit hole" that can cause you to waste valuable time. However, with a cautious approach, the internet can reveal useful information. For example, in the spray irrigation example discussed above, you can find good information from credible sources about how spray irrigation "works" to remove pollutants from the treated wastewater sprayed on a field. That information might provide helpful guidance to interpreting the sometimes dense technical information in an application.

It is important to remember, however, that you likely have limited time to become knowledgeable about a project. Deadlines may exist for when public comments are due, and once the public comment period is closed, the best researched, most persuasive public comment will not be accepted and will be for naught. Thus, you need to be cognizant of and respect deadlines in the process, and tailor your effort at becoming knowledgeable in light of the time constraints posed by such deadlines.

Checklist 3.2 at the end of this Chapter is designed to serve as a useful guide for developing background information that you can use for making public comments in the permitting process.

3.1.3 Requesting a Public Hearing

As noted in Chapter 2, public hearings on permit applications generally occur in one of two ways: DNREC decides on its own to hold a public hearing, or

DNREC allows members of the public to request a public hearing. DNREC must tell you in a public notice whether it has already decided to hold a hearing or if you must request one. Sometimes, the public hearing aspect is included in the public notice of the application, other times it is given in a second, separate public notice given at some point after the public notice of application receipt.

The first option is often used when DNREC believes there is or will be public interest in the project, and one of the ways it measures that interest is the volume of public comment it receives. The second option will lead DNREC to set a public hearing if there is "a meritorious request for a hearing within a reasonable time as stated in the advertisement." 7 Del. C. § 6004(b). To be "meritorious," the request for public hearing must "exhibit[] a familiarity with the application and a reasoned statement of the permit's probable impact." *Id.* Thus, simply asking for a public hearing is not enough; you need to show that you have read the application and are familiar with contents ("a familiarity with the application") and that you have concerns about what might happen if the permit is issued ("a reasoned statement of the permit's probable impact"). This is one place where your accumulated knowledge about the project can pay off. Further, you must request the public hearing "within a "reasonable time"—by the deadline stated in the public notice or within 15 days if no deadline is stated. Historically, if the request is timely and meritorious, DNREC will usually set and hold a public hearing.

Checklist 3.3 at the end of this Chapter is designed to serve as a useful guide for drafting a request for public hearing.

Requesting a public hearing can be helpful. As explained in Chapter 2, public hearings give you an opportunity to find out additional information if the applicant makes a presentation and DNREC (and sometimes, the applicant) make themselves available to answer questions. Public hearings can also be a place to put important information before the Secretary so that it is part of the record (though that goal can be also accomplished via submitting the information through written public comment submitted to the Hearing Officer outside the public hearing as described in the public notice). A public hearing will also result in the Hearing Officer (who conducts the hearing) issuing a Hearing Officer's Report which summarizes the hearing and responds to some of the issues raised in the public comments. This can help create a more fulsome record for purposes of appeal. As a result, you should consider whether it makes sense to request a public hearing.

Whether or not you request a public hearing, the permit process creates a key place for public input: the opportunity for public comment on the application. Effective advocacy focuses on making public comment as impactful as possible.

3-2 Making Effective Public Comments

Public comment can serve two purposes. The first is to impact a permit decision by giving the permit writer and ultimate decision maker (the Secretary) reasons to see things your way. The second is to create a record that you can use if you decide to appeal a decision because the permit writer/decision maker did not do what you wanted them to do. Recognizing that your public comment needs to serve these two purposes can help you shape your comments to be more effective.

Public comments take two forms: written and oral. Generally, you do not need to do both forms—that is, you can submit public comments in writing only, orally only, or in both forms. Because these are the two forms of public comment, it is important to consider how to be effective at each one.

3.2.1 Drafting Effective Written Comments

As an initial matter, submitting public comment in whatever form can have a positive impact. DNREC pays attention to public comments regardless of the form because the comments provide a sense of community interest and support/opposition to a project. In a case the Clinic handled, nearly 100 public comments submitted after public notice convinced DNREC that it should hold a public hearing on the application even though no member of the public requested one. Thus, submitting a comment can have an impact.

If you want to affect DNREC's decision making process, you are more likely to achieve that goal if you put some thought and effort into drafting your public comment. This section focuses on these types of written comments.

Written comments have a certain advantage to them: you take as long as you want to prepare them (subject, of course, to deadlines when they are due), you can edit them so that they say what you want to say in exactly the way you want to say it, and they have no limit to how long they can be. For this reason, written comments are a preferable form of public comment.

Preliminaries. Comments should take the form of a letter, addressed to the person who has been designated to receive public comments.[12] You should identify the matter to which your comment applies. That might just be the name of the applicant/proposed permittee, with reference to the permit for which it applied. Thus, if ABC Corporation is applying for an NPDES Permit, your comment letter can have a "Re:" line like this: "Re: Application of ABC Corp. for an NPDES Permit." If you have a Permit Number, include that: "Re: Application of ABC Corp. to Renew NPDES Permit No. DE987654321." If DNREC has already decided to hold a public hearing, or if it suspects there may be a large volume of comments, it may set up a "Docket" with a "Docket #" that is listed in the public notice. If so, use it. The whole point is that you want to make clear what you are commenting on so that DNREC can put your comment in the appropriate file. The Appendix to this Guide contains actual public comments with annotations that show you examples of how this is done.

Substance. One of the first important things you must determine before preparing your written public comment is where things are at in the permitting process. Generally, if you are submitting public comment *before* DNREC has prepared a draft or final permit, your focus is on trying to steer the initial decision a particular way. If you are commenting *after* DNREC has made an initial decision to issue a permit (in other words, you are commenting on a draft permit DNREC has prepared), you are trying to get DNREC to change its already-made decision. As you might expect, the latter of these is more difficult to achieve, and what you are likely doing is commenting in a way that is thinking ahead to an appeal.

---

[12] Public notices announcing the opportunity to comment should designate the person who will receive public comments. It might be a Hearing Officer; it might be a DNREC employee.

Although the timing matters, public comments are focused on affecting DNREC decision making (either initial or mind-changing), and so effective commenting involves recognizing what is (and what is not) likely to be persuasive.

Another factor to consider is making a comment that DNREC needs to consider carefully. Often times public comments take the form of questions: How will this project protect the environment? Will this project satisfy regulation X? Such questions—entirely legitimate—are nevertheless easy for DNREC to answer. Of course the project will protect the environment—we're making sure it does. Yes, the project will satisfy regulation X because we make sure that it does. Once the question is answered, DNREC can push the comment to the side. By contrast, a comment which takes an affirmative position—the project will not protect the environment because it lacks A, B, C—makes DNREC work harder. It has to consider whether A, B, and C will protect the environment and, if so, why they are not in the project. So think about public comments as affirmative statements that DNREC either has to accept (in which case DNREC should act the way you want them to) or has to disprove (so that the "A, B, and C" you are arguing for is somehow not necessary for satisfying the necessary legal and factual requirements.

DNREC's job is to apply the law. Usually, the application of the law does not require public approval, but instead requires consideration of the particulars of what the law requires and then making sure that those requirements are satisfied. When viewed from this perspective, DNREC is likely less moved by general statements of opposition ("This project is a bad idea") or opinion ("There are already too many of these facilities in the County"), and more likely to be moved by comments tied to DNREC's application of the law ("the permit would violate the requirements of section X of the statute/regulations").[13] Thus, effective written public comment channels general opposition or opinion into specific comments that makes DNREC consider whether its decision will apply the law correctly or not.

---

[13] This is not to say that public opposition has no place. When DNREC senses strong public opposition to a project, it seems more willing to hold a public hearing regardless of a public request in order to give the public a chance to voice its opposition. Rather, the point to emphasize here is that DNREC does not seem to make *permitting decisions* on the basis of public opposition.

With this in mind, effective written public comment involves the following:

- Reference to relevant legal provisions and principles
- Use of specific facts relevant to the project
- Argument for how (based on the facts) relevant legal requirements are not being met

Reference to Relevant Legal Provisions and Principles. Every permit DNREC issues arises out of statutory and regulatory provisions allowing DNREC to issue that permit. Those provisions usually require DNREC to do or consider things as part of the process for issuing the permit. These provisions provide a roadmap for public commentary: if DNREC is required to do or consider something when it issues this type of permit, did DNREC in fact do or consider the necessary things? If not, then DNREC is not applying the law correctly, and that is a legitimate basis for public comment (and, ultimately, a basis for challenging DNREC's decision on appeal). This is where the legal aspect of becoming knowledgeable about a project (Section 3-1.2 above) can pay off. Go through the applicable regulations and note those requirements that DNREC has failed to follow—then comment accordingly.

Sometimes, more general legal principles—based on fundamental concepts of fairness and due process—might also apply. A failure to provide notice would likely violate a specific regulatory requirement, but it might also violate a fundamental sense of fairness that is built into the law. This can also be a legitimate basis for comment.

Use of Specific Facts Relevant to the Project. Once you understand the legal requirements, you can then match up the facts with those requirements. If the regulations require that the permit applicant perform a certain analysis and it has not done so, then the fact of the failure to perform the required analysis provides the basis for a comment pointing out the requirement and the failure to satisfy the requirement. This is where the factual aspect of becoming knowledgeable about a project can pay off.

You should also consider attaching whatever documents or other materials you want DNREC to consider in connection with your comment. This puts that information before DNREC so that it will be reviewed during the final permit decision process. Attaching documents or other factual information to your comments also puts those materials into the record before the Secretary so that there is no dispute it can be used in an appeal of the Secretary's decision.

Arguments for How Relevant Legal Requirements are not Being Met. Here is where the law and facts come together into an argument: if the law requires something be done (law), and it is not being done (fact), then the legal requirement is not being satisfied, and the decision-making process is flawed.

Depending on the facts and complexity of the situation, this process of law/fact/ argument can result in numerous comments. If that is the case, it makes sense to call each instance out separately, so that your "public comment" in facts consists of several comments combined into a single document.

Included in the Appendix to this Guide are examples of public comments the Guide's author drafted and submitted to DNREC, along with annotations in light of the discussion above. These are only examples; yours may look very different, **and that's OK**. What is most important is that your comments be submitted so that they are heard and taken into consideration by DNREC.

Checklist 3.4 at the end of this Chapter is designed to serve as a useful guide for drafting written public comments. Based on the different factors described above, each set of written comments will likely be unique.

Tone. No matter how passionate you are about your position, or how wrong you think DNREC is in a particular case, the tone of your written comments should be free of anger and vitriol. Keep it calm and professional. This doesn't mean that you can't use a few well placed adjectives, but a hostile or angry tone lessens the chances that the person reading your comment will take it seriously.

AN IMPORTANT NOTE ON WRITTEN COMMENTS: No matter how brilliant a written public comment may be, it has no chance of affecting DNREC's decision if it you do not submit it in a timely way to the right person. Most public notices announcing an opportunity to submit public comment will provide a deadline for when comments are due and identify to whom you should submit the comments. PAY ATTENTION and COMPLY with those instructions in order to ensure that your written comments have a chance to impact the permit process.

3-2.2. Effective Oral Public Comments and Public Hearing Strategies

Oral public comments occur at public hearings.[14] As explained in Chapter 2's description of the public hearing process, public comment usually comes after the applicant has made any presentation it wants to make, and DNREC has made its presentation.[15] Public comment is often subject to time limits imposed by the Hearing Officer—3 or 5 minute limits are typical. Because of those time limits, oral public comments at the public hearing can only say so much because you can usually speak only 140 – 160 words a minute.

Public hearings, however, provide some opportunity to gain valuable information. If the applicant or DNREC are going to speak about the application and permit, you might be able to find out information that was not available from review of the permit file alone. This can be especially true of the applicant has some sense of public concerns and tries to preemptively address them at the

---

[14] You can show up at a public hearing and file written comments. That is sufficient to make sure they get in the record before the Secretary. It is probably best to make a short statement during the public comment time announcing that you have written comments you want to submit, and "make a record" that you are handing them to the Hearing Officer ("Mr./Ms Hearing Officer, I have some written comments which I would like to have included in the record that I am handing to you now").

[15] What does DNREC present? DNREC will always want to introduce into the hearing record things like proof of the publication of all public notices and copies of documents like the permit application and a draft permit (if one has been prepared). If there is a draft permit, DNREC may make a presentation on what the draft permit contains.

hearing. So you should view public hearings as an opportunity to gather new information.[16]

Because you are going to have limited time for oral comment, you need to be prepared ahead of the hearing. Just like with written comments, you should figure out what you want to say in your oral comments before you go to the meeting. If something comes up at the meeting, you can add a comment about it to your prepared comments. You will be less effective if you wait and try to come up with comments "on the spot."

Like written comments, focus the substance of your comments on legal and factual issues as best you can. Given the time constraints, you might want to focus on just one or two issues. If you coordinate with others attending the hearing, so that each of you is commenting on different things on your common list of concerns, you are more likely to get all those issues on the record.

One of the things you can do as part of your oral comments is ask for the comment period to be extended to some time (7, 14, 30 days) after the public hearing. This can give you time to digest what you learn at the hearing and formulate comments that raise the new issues or concerns that hearing testimony has raised in your mind.[17] Granting such requests is not automatic—you need to convince the Hearing Officer that something new or different has arisen that you could not have commented on before such that you need more time to formulate a comment. Even if you think the reason is good, the Hearing Officer might not, and therefore not extend the comment period beyond the date of the hearing.

As with written comments, the tone of your oral comments should be respectful and avoid language or volume that might cause the Hearing Officer to

---

[16] You may not have the opportunity to ask questions directly of the applicant or DNREC. Sometimes, however, the applicant or DNREC chooses to respond to comments in the hearing (say, by addressing an issue that one or more comments raised). It doesn't always happen, but this can be an indirect way to pry some additional information out of the applicant or DNREC.

[17] You should understand that, if additional time for comment is granted, your comments will have to take the form of written public comments; the Hearing Officer will not reconvene the hearing just so you can orally give your comments.

dismiss you as too “emotional” or “disruptive.” Get your points on the record. You will be dismayed by how quickly the time for comment passes.

Finally, oral and written comments are not mutually exclusive—you can do both.

Checklist 3.5 at the end of this Chapter is designed to serve as a useful guide for preparing oral public comments at a public hearing.

CHAPTER 3 CHECKLISTS

3.1 Preliminary Information Checklist

3.2 Background Research Checklist

3.3 Requesting Public Hearing Checklist

3.4 Written Public Comment Checklist

3.5 Oral Public Comment Checklist

CHECKLIST 3.1 – PRELIMINARY INFORMATION CHECKLIST

1. Get the Public Notice for the DNREC Permitting Action

Public notice is published in newspapers of "general circulation." Public Notice is also put up on DNREC's Website. Go to:

https://dnrec.alpha.delaware.gov/public-notices/

You may need to click on the different Division names (Air Quality, Waste & Hazardous, Water, Climate& Energy, Fish and Wildlife, and Other) to find the specific notice for the project you are interested in.

2. Review the Public Notice for pertinent information.

The Public Notice should provide you with information you need to plan out how you want to respond. This can include:

- Place to review the application:

  ___ Online (website:)

  ___ DNREC Office (Address:)

- Has DNREC Scheduled a public hearing or must one be requested?

  ___ Hearing already scheduled

  Date and Time:

  Location:

  ____Hearing will not be held unless meritorious request for hearing is submitted

  Deadline for submission of Request for Public Hearing:

  Where/To Whom must Request be submitted:

- Deadline for submission of Public Comments

  Date by which Public Comments must be submitted:

  How/To Whom must Public Comments be submitted:

  ___Can the Comments be submitted online through DNREC Website?

  ___Can Comments be submitted via mail?

  ___To Whom must comments be mailed?

  ___Address to mail Comments

CHECKLIST 3.2 – BACKGROUND INFORMATION CHECKLIST

1. Review the Permit Application.

Obtain or go see a copy of the Application for the permit DNREC will issue for the Project. Some preliminary information to glean from the Application

___Name and Address of Applicant:

___Location of the Project being permitted:

___Type of Permit sought (as well as citation to statute or regulation if provided):

___Description of the activity for which Permit is Sought:

___Environmental resources to be impacted by proposed activity (streams, lakes, groundwater, etc.):

2. Research the process proposed—are there aspects (emissions, by-products, waste products, discharges, other effects) of the process that cause concern?

3. Research the law—what do the statutes and regulations require be in a permit request?

4. Compare the Application to the law/regulations—does the Application provide the information required by the law and regulations?

5. Compare the process aspects (Checklist item #3) to the law/regulations—are there aspects (emissions, by-products, waste products, discharges, other effects) of the process that are prohibited or limited by the law/regulations?

6. Is there additional information—about the Applicant or the process—that can be obtained via FOIA requests of DE agencies?

___Agencies that might have information

___Each agency's FOIA process (where/to whom submit request)

___Can you get the FOIA'd information within public comment timeframe?

CHECKLIST 3.3 – REQUESTING PUBLIC HEARING CHECKLIST

1. From your review of the Public Notice (Checklist 3.1), determine to whom and by what date you must submit your request for a Public Hearing.

2. From your background information research (Checklist 3.2), prepare a short description of the following:

___The Permit applied for and the Applicant
(example: "XYZ Corp.'s application for a spray irrigation permit for a facility located hear Millsboro, DE")

___A description of what the project will do
(example: "Under the Permit, XYZ Corp. will dispose of wastewater from 12 industrial facilities by spraying it onto 300 acres of farmland located west of Millsboro")

___A description of your concerns about the proposed activity
(example: "The wastewater XYZ will spray contains pollutants that will percolate into groundwater beneath that site that is part of an aquifer providing drinking water to residents of Millsboro. The Permit needs to adequately regulate these pollutants to protect this drinking water source")

Remember, the purpose of this information is to make your request for a public hearing be "meritorious," which the statute defines as "exhibit[ing] a familiarity with the application and a reasoned statement of the permit's probable impact." 7 Del. C. § 6004(b).

3. Combine your information into a written request.

(example: "I am requesting a public hearing on the application of XYZ Corp. for a spray irrigation permit for a facility located hear Millsboro, DE. Under the Permit, XYZ Corp. will dispose of wastewater from 12 industrial facilities by spraying it onto 300 acres of farmland located west of Millsboro. The wastewater XYZ will spray contains pollutants that will percolate into groundwater beneath that site that is part of an aquifer providing drinking water to residents of Millsboro. The Permit needs to adequately regulate these pollutants to protect this drinking water source.")

4. DON'T FORGET TO SUBMIT YOUR REQUEST FOR PUBLIC HEARING TO THE RIGHT PLACE/PERSON BY THE DEADLINE!

CHECKLIST 3.4 – WRITTEN PUBLIC COMMENT CHECKLIST

1. Create an Outline of the points you want to include in your Written Public Comment.

___If you want to comment that certain statutes/regulations have not been complied with:

___compile list of the statutes/regulations and their text

___for each such regulation, prepare an explanation of how/why the application does not comply

___If you want to comment that certain adverse results will occur if the Permit is granted:

___compile a list of those adverse effects

___for each such adverse effect, prepare a short description of how/why the adverse effect will occur

___for each such adverse effect, prepare a short description of how/why the effect is adverse

___for each such adverse effect, compile any support (studies, materials from DNREC or EPA websites, etc.) that support any part of your assertions about the adverse effect

2. Start by drafting comments in form of a letter that:
- Is addressed to the person identified (from Public Notice—see Checklist 3.1)
- Identifies the matter (by Public Comment Docket # and/or by description of the permit (example: "Application for Spray Irrigation Permit by XYZ Corp.")

3. Using your Outline developed in Item #1 above, spell out each of your points in the comment letter. Generally, put what you think is your strongest point first, then repeat that until all the points in your Outline have been covered.

4. DON'T FORGET TO SUBMIT YOUR WRITTEN COMMENT TO THE RIGHT PLACE/PERSON BY THE DEADLINE!

CHECKLIST 3.5 – ORAL PUBLIC COMMENT CHECKLIST

1. Create an Outline of the points you want to include in your Oral Public Comment.

___If you want to comment that certain statutes/regulations have not been complied with:

___compile list of the statutes/regulations and their text

___for each such regulation, prepare an explanation of how/why the application does not comply

___If you want to comment that certain adverse results will occur if the Permit is granted:

___compile a list of those adverse effects

___for each such adverse effect, prepare a short description of how/why the adverse effect will occur

___for each such adverse effect, prepare a short description of how/why the effect is adverse

___for each such adverse effect, compile any support (studies, materials from DNREC or EPA websites, etc.) that support any part of your assertions about the adverse effect

2. Prepare a script or at least an outline of what you want to say in your oral comments. This will help you stay on track to raise the issues you want to raise.

3. Using your Outline developed in Item #1 above, discuss each point in your script/outline. YOU WILL LIKELY HAVE LIMITED TIME (3 – 5 minutes), and at 140 – 160 words per minute when speaking, you need to be succinct. Spell out each of your points in your script/outline. Generally, put what you think is your strongest point first, then repeat that until all the points in your Outline have been covered.

4. If you have documents you want to have considered, bring a set of the documents to the hearing so that you can submit them to the Hearing Officer.

5. Given the short amount of time generally given for oral comments, consider one or more of the following strategies:

- **Split up topics amongst several speakers so that all topics get covered**
- **Submit written comments at the public hearing in addition to your oral testimony so that all your points are covered**

6. DON'T FORGET TO ATTEND THE PUBLIC HEARING SO THAT YOU CAN PRESENT YOUR ORAL COMMENTS!

CHAPTER 4
EFFECTIVE ADVOCACY AFTER PERMIT ISSUANCE

Once the Secretary makes a final decision on a permit, disappointed persons may want to appeal that decision. This Chapter considers the issues and strategies that affect such appeals.

As noted in Chapter 2, the first level of appeal is to a quasi-judicial administrative board: the Coastal Zone Industrial Control Board for Secretary actions under the Coastal Zone Act, and the Environmental Appeals Board for all other appeals. The first question that either Board will ask is: does the person/entity filing the appeal have a legal right to stand before the Board and present the appeal—i.e., does the Appellant have standing?

4-1. Can You Appeal? The Issue of Standing

While any member of the public can submit public comments, not everyone can file an appeal of a Secretary's decision. 7 Del. C. § 6008(a) limits appeals to the EAB to "Any person whose interest is substantially affected by any action of the Secretary."[18] Delaware Courts have ruled that a person is "substantially affected" (and, therefore, has standing) if the person can show 3 things:

1. The person has suffered an "**injury-in-fact**"—that is, the person has an injury that is "imminent" (has happened or very soon will happen), "substantial" (more than just a trivial thing), "concrete" (in the sense that it can be identified and is real, not speculative), and "particularized" (is something that is different from an injury to the public at large);

2. The injury is "**fairly traceable**" to the action complained of (i.e., that the action—what the Secretary approves in the decision—will **cause** the injury); and

[18] The Coastal Zone Act uses slightly different language ("Any person aggrieved by a final decision of the Secretary . . .," 7 Del. C. § 7007(b)), but the Delaware Supreme Court has ruled that "substantially affected" and "aggrieved" have the same meaning for purposes of standing.

3. The injury is "**redressable**"—that is, the Board or a court could grant relief that would "redress" the injury by reducing or eliminating it.

In addition, if the person seeking to appeal is an organization/entity (i.e., is not a natural human being) the law imposes these additional requirements on the organization/entity for it to have standing:

1. **One or more of the organization's members** can show that he/she **has standing** (i.e., can satisfy the 3-part test outlined just above);

2. The lawsuit is **germane to the organization's purpose** (that is, the appeal is something that fits within the organization's mission and work); and

3. **Individual members are not necessary** to participate in the litigation (beyond proving individual standing as required by the 1st element of organizational standing).

If an appellant cannot satisfy the applicable test(s), the appellant does not have standing and the appeal ends without consideration of the merits of the appeal.[19]

These elements have been and regularly continue to be litigated in appeals to the EAB and CZICB.[20] By far the most common area of dispute is whether an appellant satisfies the "injury-in-fact" requirement. Recent Delaware cases have held that the cessation or diminution of enjoyment of recreational activities (like boating, kayaking, crabbing, swimming, hiking, etc.) can be enough to support a finding of injury-in-fact. Direct impacts to property and health can also support standing.

---

[19] Standing is considered "jurisdictional" because a Board is said to not have jurisdiction over an appeal if the appellant lacks standing, Without jurisdiction, the Board cannot consider the merits of the appeal. Because standing can lead to termination of an appeal without considering the merits, it is attractive to DNREC, permittees, and even the Boards to raise and decide the standing issue first. That is why so much litigation about standing takes place.

[20] The Clinic has litigated many of the recent standing cases in Delaware.

One of the first things that a potential appellant should do is think about how to prove standing. One way is to have the appellant(s) testify at the public hearing. Another is to prepare an affidavit or a declaration[21] setting out the facts that prove standing, and present those affidavit(s) and declaration(s) as exhibits at the hearing. Examples of Declarations used to prove standing (with personal information redacted) are included in the Appendix. Whether live testimony or affidavit/declaration, you want to make sure that all facts you can muster are included to support standing so that those facts become part of the record before the Secretary.

Checklist 4.1 at the end of this Chapter is designed to generate information that can be helpful for proving standing. The Appendix of Standing Declarations help to show how the information from the Checklist exercise can be put into a form to prove standing.

As this discussion suggests, the issue of standing can be complex, and efforts to establish standing may benefit from legal assistance. The Clinic has litigated many of the recent standing cases in Delaware.

4-2. Initiating Appeals of Secretary Decisions

Assuming one has standing (or a good faith basis to believe it), one initiates an appeal by filing a "Statement of Appeal" (to the EAB) or a "Notice of Appeal"

---

[21] The difference between affidavits and declarations rests on the manner in which the affiant/declarant proves the truth of the assertions contained in the document. An affidavit is a document in which the affiant (person whose affidavit it is and who is making the statements in the affidavit) signs the document before a notary who has placed the affiant under oath. In a sense, the affidavit is "sworn testimony"—the affiant swears or affirms the truth of the assertions in the document, and the notary signs and seals the affidavit attesting that the affiant made the statements in the document. Affidavits therefore require the involvement of a notary—some of whom charge for notarizing the document. A Declaration is a statement that a person signs "under penalty of perjury"—that is, by signing the declarant acknowledges that he/she could be charged with making a false statement/perjury of anything said in the document is not true. Declarations do not need a notary—only the language to make clear it is being signed under penalty of perjury. That makes them easier to finalize. The threat of a perjury charge—which exists when you swear to the accuracy of the affidavit before a notary or sign "under penalty of perjury"—is designed to function like swearing on the Bible does at trial (because, the law presumes, you would not tell a lie before God after invoking him via the Bible).

(to the CZICB). It is important to remember the tight timeframes for appeals discussed in Chapter 2 (20 days for appeals to the EAB, 14 days for appeals to the CZICB).[22]

The EAB's regulations require specific things to be in the Statement of Appeal. It must be "in the form of a written statement" and set forth:

- "the interest which has been substantially affected;"
- "an allegation that the decision is improper;"
- "the reasons why the decision is improper;" and
- "an estimate of the number of witnesses and the time involved in presenting the appeal at the public hearing."

The regulations also require that a $50 check, payable to the Environmental Appeals Board, be included with the Statement of Appeal.

The effect of these requirements is that the Statement of Appeal needs to be detailed and specific. Thus, drafting a Statement of Appeal should involve putting all of the issues into the Statement that you want to raise on appeal. Completeness (in the sense of including all issues you think you might want to raise) is important, as the Board might exclude testimony and argument on issues not raised in the Statement of Appeal. As a result, you need to think ahead to the hearing when drafting the Statement. As a result, you need to be careful and inclusive when initiating your appeal.

The CZICB does not have formal requirements like the EAB, but generally wants similar information included and will limit an appellant to what is in the Notice filed. As the example in the Appendix shows, the CZICB will accept a

[22] Note as well that the time does not stop running until the Board receives the actual appeal. You therefore need to think about the time it takes to mail or deliver the document when calculating your "deadline" for appeal.

form to which the details of the bases for appeal are attached, but the form need not be used. Note that a $100 fee is required with the Notice of Appeal.

Checklist 4.2 at the end of this Chapter is designed to serve as a guide for preparing appeals. The Appendix includes two annotated notices—a Statement of Appeal filed with the EAB and a Notice of Appeal filed with the CZICB—to help illustrate how these requirements play out.

Keep in mind that an appeal to the EAB or CZICB is subject to tight timeframes: an appeal to the EAB must be received by the EAB within 20 days of the date of the Secretary's Order or public notice (whichever is later), while appeals to the CZICB must be received within 14 days of the Secretary's Order or public notice. "Received" really does mean that it is in the hands of the Board by that deadline; if it is not "received," the appeal is untimely and will not be heard. You should consider getting proof of receipt (the green Return Card with Certified Mail, a FedEx/UPS/US Postal Service Confirmation receipt) that proves when it got to where it needed to go.

The Boards allow individuals to represent themselves before the Board (what is sometimes called "*pro se*" representation because the appellant speaks for him/herself). However, organizations can only appear before the Boards through a Delaware attorney. Given the complexity of the requirements to initiate the appeal, and the issues related to conducting a public hearing, individuals may want to consider having legal representation in an appeal.

4-3. Preparing for the Board Hearing

By statute, both the EAB and the CZICB are required to hold a public hearing on an appeal filed with the Board. *See* 7 Del C. § 6008(b) (EAB "shall hold a public hearing"); 7 Del. C. §§ 7007(b) and (c) ((b): CZICB "must hold a hearing;" (c) CZICB "shall hold a public hearing"). Given the CZICB's 60-day window in which to hold the hearing and issue its written opinion, proceedings before that Board move very rapidly to hearing. By contrast, the EAB has only a 180 day requirement to complete the hearing, 7 Del. C. § 6007(c), with the ability of the parties to agree to a longer period of time. As a result, the EAB's regulations mandate certain actions happen before the hearing.

The biggest pre-hearing requirement of the EAB is that the parties must hold a "pre-hearing conference" with the Board's counsel at least 20 days before the hearing itself. As a prelude to the pre-hearing conference, the parties are required to exchange a list of witnesses and exhibits 10 days before the pre-hearing conference. The conference itself then serves as a way for the parties to try to resolve any issues or objections about exhibits or witnesses and narrow issues that the Board needs to hear.[23] Sometimes, the parties can agree on certain facts so that there does not need to be testimony about those facts. These agreements are often captured in a Stipulation of Facts signed by all the parties. The Appendix contains two examples of Stipulations of Facts before the respective Boards.[24]

The effect of these deadlines connected to the pre-hearing conference is that an appellant must finalize the plan for the hearing well in advance, as the EAB may well exclude from the hearing witnesses and exhibits that were not identified for the pre-hearing conference.[25]

With the contours of the hearing set by the pre-trial conference, you must do three things to complete your preparation:

- Make copies of your exhibits and provide them to the Board (10 copies) plus a copy to DNREC and any other parties to the appeal;

---

[23] An example of this occurred in an appeal brought be the Clinic on behalf of 99 individuals. Because the appellants presented more than 70 Declarations to show standing, counsel for DNREC agreed that DNREC would not challenge the standing of the appellants, thereby removing that issue from the hearing.

[24] Note that, in the case before the CZICB, the document serves many purposes in addition to stipulation of facts (such as specifying the parties' contentions/arguments) and takes the form of an order signed by the Board Chair. The focus here is on the stipulation of facts agreed to by all the parties.

[25] Likely because of the compressed 60-day window for decision, the CZICB does not have a formal requirement for a pre-hearing conference. However, the Board has in the past issued a "Scheduling Order" that imposed requirements on the parties requiring many of the same things as the EAB pre-hearing conference regulations require. Parties would need to comply with the Order's terms.

- Prepare the testimony of the witnesses who will testify as part of your case; and

- Prepare the cross-examination of the witnesses identified by DNREC and the other parties to the appeal.

In preparing your presentation, you must remember that the Board requires the appellant to prove that the Secretary's decision was arbitrary, capricious, or contrary to law. Chapter 60 describes it this way: "The burden of proof is upon the appellant to show that the Secretary's decision is not supported by the evidence on the record before the Board." 7 Del. C. § 6008(b). This is not an easy burden to meet, so the testimony and exhibits must be targeted to meeting this burden.

Another consideration impacting hearing preparation is that, at least according to the EAB's Regulations, an appellant is supposedly limited: "Appellants other than permit applicants or an alleged violator may only introduce evidence which was before the Secretary." 7 Del. Admin. C. 105 § 5.3. There is an unresolved legal issue relating to this restriction given that it appears to contradict other portions of the regulations and does not apply to DNREC or a permittee (thereby raising due process and equal protection concerns), but that legal issue has not yet been resolved by a Delaware court. It is therefore possible that the Board would restrict what an appellant can present to evidence that was before the Secretary. For this reason, anyone who thinks he/she might want to appeal a decision **must put as much information into the record as possible during the public comment process.** In other words, even before an appeal is filed, advocates should be thinking about the possibility of an appeal and building a record that can help if and when an appeal is filed.

Finally, in addition to this hearing preparation, the Boards usually want each party to provide some kind of Memorandum explaining their position and arguments ahead of the hearing so that the Board understands what arguments the parties will present and what the parties think the evidence will show. These pre-hearing memoranda allow each party to "preview" its case, so preparing such a memorandum requires you to marshal your facts and law into the argument you want the Board to hear. The Appendix contains examples of such pre-hearing filings.

4-4. Participating in the Board Hearing

The public hearing is a somewhat formal affair that, in some ways, looks like a trial in a court, but with different ground rules. Generally, the Board sits on a dias while the parties present their witnesses and evidence. As explained in Chapter 2, the order of presentation is usually the following:

- Opening statements/arguments by each party
- Appellant's presentation of its case (witnesses, evidence)
- Permittee's presentation of its case
- DNREC's presentation of its case
- Rebuttal evidence (if any) of the parties
- Closing arguments by each party

During this process, certain unique rules apply. First, strict rules of evidence do not apply (though parties—especially those represented by attorneys—will often make objections based on the rules of evidence). As the EAB's regulations put it: "Strict rules of evidence shall not apply. All evidence having probative value commonly accepted by a reasonably prudent person in the conduct of his or her affairs shall be admitted." 7 Del. Admin. C. 105 § 5.4. Second, after a party presents testimony of a witness, the other parties get a chance to cross-examine the witness by asking questions as well. Third, after the cross-examination (and any follow up by the party that put the witness on), the Board gets to ask questions of the witness. Sometimes, the Board's questioning prompts one or more parties to ask follow up questions. This continues until the parties' and Board's question have all been answered, then the witness is dismissed, and the next witness called.

Given this process, a party must be prepared to ask the questions that help its case. If you are presenting a witness, you need to have your initial questions prepared and ready before the hearing. Practicing with the witness can be helpful. You also need to be listening to what the witness says so that you can ask follow up questions (or, if the witness is for another party, to ask cross-examination questions). *Everything* that is said is taken down by a court reporter who will ultimately produce a transcript of the hearing.

Once all the parties have presented their respective cases, the Board may hear closing arguments. The Board will then go into executive session to deliberate its decision. The EAB will leave the hearing room, but the CZICB stops the court reporter from transcribing (this is called "going off the record") and deliberates in public. Once the Board reaches a decision, the hearing goes back into session on the record, and the Board entertains a motion for the Board to make its decision. The Board votes, and—except for CZICB hearings[26]—the hearing adjourns.

As this description suggests, participation in a public hearing requires a significant amount of preparation and the ability to think on your feet as the hearing unfolds. While an individual party can represent themselves in a hearing, legal representation might help advance one's cause better at the hearing.

4-5. Appealing the Board's Decision

Both the EAB and CZICB are subject to the requirements of Delaware's Administrative Procedures Act, 20 Del. C. §10101 *et seq*. The APA requires that the Board memorialize its decision in a written final order that contains

(1) A brief summary of the evidence;

(2) Findings of fact based upon the evidence;

[26] The CZICB—likely in response to the language in 7 Del. C. § 7007(c) mandating that the Board hold a public hearing on appeals at which "the public may attend and be heard"—allows oral public comment as part of the hearing. In practice, what often happens is that the Board reaches its decision first, and then conducts the public comment session. Of course, many of the commenters who came to urge the Board to rule one way or the other end up making comments urging a particular result *after* the decision has already been made.

(3) Conclusions of law;

(4) Any other conclusions required by law of the agency; and

(5) A concise statement of the agency's determination or action on the case.

29 Del. C. § 10128(b). The EAB has 90 days after the hearing ends to issue its final order; the CZICB has only what's left of its 60 day window to issue its final order. Perhaps because of these deadlines, final orders tend to be long on summaries of the evidence (#1), and short on most everything else (especially #2 – 4).

The right to appeal a Board decision arises only after the Board issues its final order (even though it may have announced its decision earlier at the conclusion of the public hearing). Appeals of both the EAB and the CZICB are to the Superior Court. However, the deadlines for filing an appeal differ; decisions of the EAB must be appealed within 30 days, 7 Del. C. § 6009(a), while decisions of the CZICB must be appealed in 20 days. 7 Del. C. § 7008.

Appeals to the Superior Court (whether from an EAB or CZICB decision) commence with the filing of a Notice of Appeal with the Superior Court. Rule 72 of the Rules of the Superior Court require that the Notice of Appeal be filed within the time period allowed for filing (30 days for appeals from the EAB, 20 days for appeals from the CZICB), and need to:

- specify the parties taking the appeal;
- designate the order being appealed;
- state the grounds of the appeal;
- name the Court to which the appeal is taken; and
- be signed by the attorney representing the appellants.

The document need not be long (unlike the EAG's requirements of specificity in the grounds for appeal, a summary statement that the Board's decision was arbitrary, capricious, not supported by the record, and/or contrary to law can be sufficient). The Appendix to the Guide contains an example of a Notice of Appeal.

While the last of the requirements is not iron-clad—a person can file an appeal *pro se*—legal representation in an appeal is generally a good idea. Part of the reason why is that the Superior Court requires that appeals be conducted in certain ways. It involves a structure and language that is not easy to understand. For example, briefs must be filed at certain times, containing certain specified sections, and cannot be longer than a specified number of pages or words. While courts give some leeway to *pro se* litigants, that leeway only goes so far. This does not mean that a *pro se* litigant cannot succeed—they can. Rather, the point is that it is not easy to do it on your own.

Appeals to the Superior Court are based on the record before the Board—that is, you cannot bring up evidence that you did not present to the Board except in highly unusual and very limited circumstances. As 7 Del. C. § 6009(b) (governing appeals of EAB decisions) puts it, "The Board's findings of fact shall not be set aside unless the Court determines that the records contain no substantial evidence that would reasonably support the findings. If the Court finds that additional evidence should be taken, the Court may remand the case to the Board for completion of the record." Similarly, 7 Del. C. 7008 (governing appeals from the CZICB) states: "the appeal shall be based on the record of proceedings before the Board, the only issue being whether the Board abused its discretion in applying standards set forth by this chapter and regulations issued pursuant thereto to the facts of the particular case." Thus, the appeal of a Board's decision rests on and is restricted to the evidence presented to the Board—creating the imperative that you must put everything you might want a Court on appeal to consider before the Board during the public hearing.

Note as well that the Court gives some deference to what the Board found. "No substantial evidence" generally means that if there is some evidence in the record to support the decision, that is good enough; "abuse of discretion" implies some similar deference. As a result, challenging the Board's decision on the facts is tough. By contrast, the appellate approach to questions of law (i.e., did the Board get and apply the law correctly?) is different; questions of law are reviewed "*de novo*"—meaning that the court starts with a fresh look and without deference to how the Board interpreted the law. Generally, challenges to Board decisions on the law have a greater chance of success precisely for this reason. However, it means that an appellant must be able to show the legal error in the Board's analysis.

As noted before, decisions of the Superior Court can be appealed to the Delaware Supreme Court within 30 days of the Superior Court's decision. That Court has its own rules governing such appeals, and its focus is simply on whether the Superior Court ruled improperly.

CHAPTER 4 CHECKLISTS

4.1 Standing Checklist

4.2 Notice of Appeal Checklist

CHECKLIST 4.1 – STANDING CHECKLIST

1. Identify Who will provide Standing for the Appeal.

- **If you are bringing the appeal directly on your own behalf, <u>You</u> must show that you have standing**
- **If the appeal will be brought by a group or organization, one (or preferably more) members must show that each has standing**

2. For each person who will show standing, identify whether that person has any of the following and list the ones he/she has:

- **Some negative economic impact (loss of economic value or money) that has or will result from the permitted activity**

- **Any recreational interest (hiking, canoeing/kayaking/sailing/ paddleboarding, camping, swimming, crabbing, birdwatching, etc.) that has been or will be done less or enjoyed less as a result of the permitted activity**

- **Any aesthetic interest (viewing nature) that has been or will be done less or enjoyed less as a result of the permitted activity**

- **Any personal health interest that has been or will be made worse as a result of the permitted activity**

3. For each of the interests identified in #2 above, develop an explanation of how and why the permitted activity has caused or will cause the negative effect on that interest

4. If the appellant is an organization, develop a statement of how an appeal of the permit decision is consistent with the Organization's purpose.

CHECKLIST 4.2 – NOTICE OF APPEAL CHECKLIST

1. Obtain and read a copy of the Secretary's Order issuing the Permit. Identify:

- **All grounds/reasons Secretary offers to support the decision**
- **Whether Secretary discusses grounds/issues raised in your or other's public comments**

2. Review the issues you identified in your outline for public comments (Checklist 3.4) and identify all issues that you think the Secretary ignored or did not address correctly in the Secretary's Order. (You should review other public comments if available to see if there are any other issues which you did not identify). This list will serve as the list of grounds you want to raise in your Notice of Appeal.

3. IF YOU ARE APPEALING A COASTAL ZONE ACT STATUS OR PERMITTING DECISION BY THE SECRETARY:

A. Obtain a copy of the appeal form to fill out (*see* Appendix example). If you cannot obtain a form, you can prepare a form that tracks what the form in the Appendix does.

B. Fill in the information required by the form.

C. Prepare as an attachment to the form the list of all the issues/reasons you think the Secretary's Order is in error. Remember, error can occur in application of the law or in the use of (or failure to use) relevant facts. Be as thorough as you can in your list.

D. Include the $100 fee, payable to the CZICB, with your form.

E. MAIL OR DELIVER THE COMPLETED FORM TO THE CZICB SO THAT IT IS RECEIVED WITHIN 14 DAYS OF THE SECRETARY'S ORDER. (The CZICB is located at DNREC's Dover Headquarters: 89 Kings Highway, Dover, DE 19901). You should consider getting proof of delivery (Certified Mail Return Receipt, FedEX/UPS Confirmation to prove receipt. (If you deliver personally, you can prepare a declaration proving the circumstances of the delivery).

4. IF YOU ARE APPEALING ANY OTHER FINAL DECISION BY THE SECRETARY (that is, a decision NOT under the CZA):

A. Prepare a Statement of Appeal in the form of a letter to the EAB (*see* Appendix example). (The EAB is located at DNREC's Dover Headquarters: 89 Kings Highway, Dover, DE 19901).

B. Make sure your Statement of Appeal letter includes the required elements:

1. a description of "the interest which has been substantially affected." For this, you should provide a summary statement of the basis for standing.

2. "an allegation that the decision is improper." This can be a conclusory statement (because the detailed reasons will follow in the next section). The general recognized grounds for reversing a Secretary's Order is that the decision is arbitrary, capricious, or contrary to law.

3. "the reasons why the decision is improper." In this section, you need to detail all the reasons you identified in Steps 1 and 2 above. Provide some explanation. The Appendix example should give you some idea of what this entails.

4. "an estimate of the number of witnesses and the time involved in presenting the appeal at the public hearing." Here, you want to give your best estimate. Count as witnesses the people who will establish standing (on the presumption that each will have to testify), plus any other witnesses you might want to call to support one or more of the reasons why the decision is improper. Time needed is always a guess, but for a rule of thumb assume that standing witnesses take 30 minutes and any other witness can take up to an hour (sometimes more, if he/she is an expert and/or has a lot of ground to cover).

C. You must include a $50 check, payable to the Environmental Appeals Board, with your Statement of Appeal.

D. MAIL OR DELIVER THE COMPLETED FORM TO THE EAB SO THAT IT IS RECEIVED WITHIN 20 DAYS OF THE SECRETARY'S ORDER. You should consider getting proof of delivery (Certified Mail Return Receipt, FedEX/UPS Confirmation to prove receipt. If you deliver personally, you can prepare a declaration proving the circumstances of the delivery).

INDEX OF TERMS

APPENDIX

TABLE OF CONTENTS

APPENDIX TAB 1

Annotations on Sheet following the Comment Document

Widener University
Delaware Law School

Environmental & Natural Resources Law Clinic
Kenneth T. Kristl, Professor of Law and Director

August 17, 2019

List Vest [1]
Hearing Officer
Department of Natural Resources and Environmental Control
89 Kings Highway
Dover, DE 19901

Re: Docket # 2019-P-W-0016 — Public Comment #1: Public Notice Issues [2]

Dear Hearing Officer Vest:

I am submitting this comment separately to raise an issue concerning the public notice and public record in connection with the above-referenced Docket.

At least one DNREC website page concerning this Docket reference that there are draft permits for both the Allen Harim and the Artesian Wastewater Management applications. *See* https://dnrec.alpha.delaware.gov/2019/07/31/public-hearing-allen-harim-on-site-wastewater-treatment-and-disposal-system-permit-application-and-artesian-wastewater-management-spray-irrigation-permit-application/ [3]

which states (emphasis supplied):

> For additional information on the above matters, and to review these applications **and draft permits** online, visit de.gov/dnrechearings or contact John Rebar, Jr., Division of Water, Groundwater Discharges Section, 89 Kings Highway, Dover, DE, 19901; by phone at 302-739-9948; or, by email, at John.Rebar@delaware.gov.
>
> Persons wishing to comment on the above applications **and draft permits** may do so either orally or in written form at the public hearing on August 21, 2019. In lieu of attending the public hearing, written comment may be submitted to the Hearing Officer via the online comment form at dnrec.alpha.delaware.gov/public-hearings/comment-form/ or via USPS to the following address:
>
> Lisa A. Vest, Hearing Officer
> Office of the Secretary
> Department of Natural Resources and Environmental Control
> 89 Kings Highway, Dover, DE 19901

However, the DNREC web page containing the documents related to these two permit requests does not contain draft permits for either application request but only the application documents. [4]

Widener University Delaware Law School, 4601 Concord Pike, Wilmington, DE 19803-0406
t: 302-477-2053 f: 302-477-2032 e: ktkristl@widener.edu delawarelaw.widener.edu

It would seem there are three possibilities here:

(1) There are no draft permits for either application;

(2) There is a draft permit for one but not the other application;

(3) There are draft permits for both applications.

If possibility #1 is true, then the references to draft permits are simply wrong, and the only documents currently available are the application packages themselves. This would mean that the August 21 hearing and the public comment period set to close on that date are solely focused on what the applications say, and that DNREC plans to use the information and comments to draft the permits. If that is the case, then I request that DNREC make available for public review and comment the draft permits when completed so that the public has an opportunity to comment on those drafts and add to the record before the Secretary. Failure to do so would deprive the public of the right to create a full record—and members of the public or the applicants could be deprived of the ability to raise issues about those permits on appeal to the EAB if the Board decides to enforce its Rule 5.3(g) limiting appellants to presenting information that was before the Secretary. [5]

If possibilities #2 or #3 are true, and there are draft permits for either or both Allen Harim and Artesian, then DNREC's failure to provide those draft is unfair and it is a violation of Delaware law to require the public to comment on those documents in meaningful way by the August 21 hearing and comment deadline, now only three working days away. I request that, if such draft permits exist, DNREC:

1. Provide copies of the draft permits to the public on the DNREC website alongside the permit application packages already there;
2. Continue the public hearing until the public has had at least 30 days to review the draft permits before such hearing is held; and [6]
3. Leave open the public comment period until at least 30 days after the draft permits are posted online.

Failure to make the draft permits available with meaningful opportunity to review and comment on those permits makes any final decision on the permits subject to challenge on public notice, procedural, and constitutional due process grounds.

Thank you for the opportunity to submit this public comment.

Sincerely,

/s/ Kenneth T. Kristl, Esq.

ANNOTATIONS FOR APPEXDIX TAB 1

[1] Addressed to the person designated to receive comments

[2] Identify the proceeding to which the comment applies. In this instance, DNREC had set up a Public Docket, and so the reference is to the Public Docket #

[3] Giving facts related to the factual issue–here, that the public notices said a draft permit existed, but [4] no draft permits had been made available to the public

[5] Explain the legal problem

[6] Suggest what DNREC should do about it.

NOTE: As a result of this comment, DNREC reached out and informed the author that draft permits were coming, that the permits would be announced at the August 21, 2019 public hearing, and that the public comment period would be extended 30 days so the public could comment on the draft permits.

APPENDIX TAB 2

Annotations on Sheet following the Comment Document

Widener University
Delaware Law School

Environmental & Natural Resources Law Clinic
Kenneth T. Kristl, Professor of Law and Director

September 16, 2019

Lisa Vest
Hearing Officer [1]
Department of Natural Resources and Environmental Control
89 Kings Highway
Dover, DE 19901

Re: Docket # 2019-P-W-0016 — Public Comment Set #2: Operating Permit Issues [2]

Dear Hearing Officer Vest:

I am submitting these comments concerning the Operating Permit Applications submitted by Allen Harim and Artesian Wastewater Management ("Artesian") which have been combined together in the above-referenced Docket.

[3]

Comment 1. The record from the Construction Permit granted to Artesian (pursuant to Secretary's Order No. 2017-W-0029) and the Construction Permit granted to Allen Harim should be included in their entirety in the Record of this Docket.

I represented Keep Our Wells Clean, Gail Salomon, Yauheniya Zialenskaya, Uladzislau I. Navitski, Thomas DiOrio, Lynn Taylor-Miller, Charlie Miller, and Virginia Weeks in an appeal to the Environmental Appeals Board (EAB No. 2017-14) of the Construction Permit granted to Artesian as a result of Secretary's Order No. 2017-W-0029. In that appeal, Appellants wanted to raise issues about how the system would operate as a way to measure the adequacy of the design being constructed. Both DNREC's and Artesian's argued that those issues were not appropriate at the construction permit stage because they would be handled in the operating permits to be issued to Allen Harim and Artesian. In fact, the EAB granted motions *in limine*, orally ruling that "such that evidence presented must be limited to evidence before the Secretary that speaks to proper site selection and system design *and not the operations of the plant*."[1] This Public Docket concerns Allen Harim's and Artesian's applications for, and now DNREC's drafts of, those operating permits, and thus the representations and promises of DNREC and Artesian at the public hearings and in various documents from the construction permit stage are relevant in order to determine whether in fact those representations were accurate and the promises were kept. Further, 7 Del. Admin. C. 7101 § 6.5.3.1 requires an operation permit application

[4]

[1] May 22, 2018 Hearing Transcript at 167 (emphasis supplied). A copy of the May 22, 2018 and March 12, 2019 Hearing Transcripts before the EAB in 2017-14 are being provided with these comments to assure they are part of the record before the Secretary. Please note that, because of the size of the files for the various documents cited in these comments, I am submitting these comments electronically in the Docket without the digital files, and mailing a hard copy of the comments with the documents attached.

[5]

Widener University Delaware Law School, 4601 Concord Pike, Wilmington, DE 19803-0406
t: 302-477-2053 f: 302-477-2032 e: ktkristl@widener.edu delawarelaw.widener.edu

to include a "Design Engineer Inspection Report(s) certifying the facility has been constructed in accordance with approved plans and specifications" (6.5.3.1.3) and that a set of "as-built" drawings bearing a Professional Engineer's seal be submitted (6.5.2.1.9). The only way to assure those requirements are being met is to refer back to the construction permits and its associated application documents. While my public comments here will refer to and attach some of the documents from that construction permit appeal record, all documents before the Secretary on Artesian's and Allen Harim's construction permits and the EAB appeal of Artesian's construction permit must be considered part of the record before the Secretary on these operating permits.

Comment 2. The Allen Harim and Artesian Applications should be treated as linked together.

The construction permit granted in Secretary's Order 2017-W-0029 and at issue in EAB no. 2017-14 was an amendment to a permit granted Artesian in 2013. The Original 2013 version of the permit envisioned Artesian constructing a wastewater treatment plant to treat domestic wastewater and then spray that treated wastewater on certain fields. The permit amendment sought by Artesian and granted by DNREC removed the Artesian treatment component in "Phase I," shifting that treatment to Allen Harim. As stated in Artesian's May 5, 2017 Amended Design Development Report,

> Phase I of the project is to construct a storage lagoon and disposal spray fields, and to accept treated wastewater effluent from [Allen Harim]. The design average daily flow is 1.5 MGD with a peak flow of 2.0 MGD . . . [6]

May 5, 2017 Amended DDR at p. 5.[2] Later, the May 5, 2017 Amended DDR states:

> Phase 1 does not include any untreated wastewater entering the ANSRWRF facility. The influent to the storage lagoon will have been treated by the existing wastewater treatment facility on the Allen Harim site . . .

May 5, 2017 Amended DDR at p. 24.

The draft permit for Artesian in this Docket confirms this approach in that it contains no requirements for the treatment of wastewater at the Artesian facility. As the General Description section on page 6 of the Artesian Permit puts it:

> This Permit authorizes the operation of Phase I only. Phase I of the project consisted of the construction of a storage lagoon and disposal spray fields, and to accept treated wastewater effluent from Allen Harim Foods, LLC (Allen Harim).

---

[2] A copy of the May 5, 2017 Amended DDR is being provided with the physical copy of these comments to assure it is part of the record before the Secretary.

The Artesian Draft Permit cements this interdependence when it allows for the measurement of the quality of the influent to ANSRWRF to be determined by sampling "in accordance with" Allen Harim's operating permit. Draft Permit Part II A. Monitoring Requirements 1. Influent Monitoring Requirements (page 14 of 34). Further, in Part I C. Sprayed Effluent Limitations (page 9 of 34), the Permit imposes limits on the pH, Total Residual Chlorine, Chloride and Sodium, but specifically states for each of these that "[t]he point of compliance shall be at Allen Harim's effluent pump station." *Id.* at ¶¶ 6 – 9.

Thus, the effectiveness of Artesian's spray irrigation operation depends upon the effectiveness of Allen Harim's treatment of the wastewater, as Artesian cannot treat non-compliant wastewater at its Phase I facility.[3] As a result, Artesian's compliance with the regulations relating to spray irrigation is inextricably tied to Allen Harim's wastewater treatment performance. The two operating permits applied for in this Docket must be viewed, treated, and issued together. If one permit is denied, or cannot be issued, then the other permit should be not be issued.

Comment 3. The Allen Harim Application Documents Do Not Conform With The Regulations.

As the Allen Harim application and the public notices issued by DNREC shows, Allen Harim is applying for an Operating Permit for an Onsite Wastewater Treatment and Disposal System. It is therefore governed by, *inter alia*, 7 Del. Admin. C. 7101 § 6.5.3. Section 6.5.3.1 sets forth the requirements for an operations permit application, including the requirements that the application include a "Design Engineer Inspection Report(s) certifying the facility has been constructed in accordance with approved plans and specifications" (6.5.3.1.3) and that a set of "as-built" drawings bearing a Professional Engineer's seal be submitted (6.5.2.1.9). [7]

Presumably to satisfy 6.5.3.1.3's requirement of certification of completion of construction, Artesian application includes a letter dated **March 8, 2017** from Adam Zimmerman, P.E. at Reid Engineering. Mr. Zimmerman's letter states that Reid Engineering completed a Final Completion Site Visit on **January 10, 2017,** and based on that visit, certified that the construction work was completed "in accordance with the Construction Documents and approved revisions." These dates are important because, to my knowledge, on January 10, 2017, Allen Harim had not finalized any plan to end its NPDES discharge to Beaver Creek and send its treated wastewater to ANSRWRF. In fact, in the EAB No. 2017-14 appeal of Artesian's Construction Permit, Artesian presented as its Exhibit 5 an incomplete copy of a Process Wastewater Services Agreement between Artesian and Allen Harim **dated January 27, 2017**[4] in which Allen Harim expresses (for the first time) that it "wants Artesian to provide disposal services with respect to industrial and/or process wastewater" and the parties agree (for the first time)

[3] While the Artesian Operating Permit application mentions an ability to disinfect wastewater in the 90-million gallon storage lagoon, nothing suggests that Artesian plans to or could treat for all the pollutants that are expected to be in the Allen Harim wastewater that will be sent to Artesian.

[4] I am providing a copy of Artesian's Exhibit 5 in EAB No. 2017-14 with the physical copy of these comments to assure it is part of the record before the Secretary.

that "Owner [Allen Harim], and not Artesian, will be primarily responsible for treating any industrial or process wastewater, or storm water, that is discharged from Owner's Property . . . ." Agreement p. 1. This chronology strongly suggests (if not outright proves) that whatever Allen Harim finished constructing on January 10, 2017 could not possibly represent a design formulated pursuant to an agreement Allen Harim entered three weeks later. In other words, Allen Harim has supplied a certification **for an old plan of construction, not the current plan for which it seeks operating permit approval.**

Further evidence of this chronology problem exists in the "As Built" Drawing submitted with the Operating Permit Application. The Drawing itself is on Artesian Wastewater Management Paper, and bears the seal of Daniel Konstanski, P.E., who works for Artesian (*see* cover of May 5, 2017 Amended DDR), not Reid Engineering. The earliest date on the "As Built" drawing is **May 10, 2017**, with revisions until October 24, 2017, and Mr. Konstanski's first seal is dated **October 26, 2017**. The Drawing also shows additional items in red, with a second seal by Mr. Konstanski in red dated **March 13, 2019**. In short, what Allen Harim is now proposing to operate could not have been completely built by January 10, 2017 as claimed in Mr. Zimmerman's letter if changes to what was "As Built" were occurring after the March 2017 date of the Zimmerman letter. As such, the Allen Harim Application does not satisfy 6.5.3.1.3.[5]

This is not the only example of Allen Harim relying upon pre-Artesian conditions or facts in attempting to justify a post-Artesian operating permit. The Application materials also include a "Design Engineer's Report" that is dated (according to the Engineer's signature) **November 23, 2015**—a date more than a year before Allen Harim and Artesian reached their agreement to send the Allen Harim Wastewater to ANSRWRF. The design components appear to include the additional nitrogen and other pollutant removal that Allen Harim is supposedly abandoning in favor of sending its water to ANSRWRF.[6] In short, it is out of date and not reflective of what is now proposed.[7] Allen Harim's

---

[5] Allen Harim cannot point to the Konstanski seals as satisfying the requirement of § 6.5.3.1.3. Neither seal comes with language "certifying the facility has been constructed in accordance with approved plans and specifications" as required by the regulation. In fact, Mr. Konstanski's March 13, 2019 certification seems to disavow any claim of accuracy, as it comes with the disclaimer that "This Record Drawing, reflecting changes in the work made during construction, is based on data furnished by the Contractor(s) to the Engineer. **The Engineer shall not be held responsible for the accuracy or completeness of the information provided by the contractor**" (emphasis supplied). Given this disclaimer, it appears that the drawing itself also does not satisfy the requirement of § 6.5.3.1.9.

[6] As just one example, the 2015 Design Engineer Report describes an "Anoxic Reactor #3 (New)" (*see* 2015 Design Engineer Report p. 36) which does not appear on the Process Design Chart in the Draft Permit or in the process description in the Allen Harim O&M Plan. According to the 2015 DER, this Reactor was included in the design because "Nitrate nitrogen concentration must be reduced to approximately 1.0 mg/L or less in order for the final effluent total nitrogen concentration to be $\leq$ 4.0 mg/L including approximately 1.0 mg/L ammonia nitrogen and approximately 2.0 mg/L of organ nitrogen in the final effluent TSS," 2015 Design Engineer Report p. 36—nitrogen levels which are not mandated in the Artesian or Allen Harim documents.

[7] This 2015 Design Engineer Report presents a second regulatory problem: According to § 6.5.1.4, "Once approved by the Department, the Design Engineer Report becomes the basis of the design for the project. Once a facility is permitted, **the facility must be constructed, operated and maintained in accordance with the Design Engineer Report**" (emphasis supplied). Given the apparent changes in the design since 2015 due to the decision to send treated wastewater to ANSRWRF

O&M Plan includes references to discharges to Beaverdam Creek (*see* O&M Plan at p. 19: "The Outfall 001 discharges treated wastewater into Beaverdam Creek just beyond the fence in back of the wastewater treatment plant")—even though the Draft Permit bars discharges to the Creek. Draft Permit Part I M. Schedule of Compliance a. ii (page 10 of 17). The O&M Plan's discussion of monitoring makes reference to NPDES Permit requirements (*see, e.g.*, O&M Plan p. 44) when arguably NPDES may no longer apply once wastewater is sent to ANSRWRF instead of being discharged to Beaverdam Creek. Given that the draft Allen Harim Permit requires Allen Harim to "operate . . . in accordance with the approved Operation and Maintenance Plan (O&M Plan)," Draft Permit Special Condition j (p. 16 of 17), it appears that the draft permit locks at least some of these errors into place. One gets the distinct impression that Allen Harim simply reused documents from its 2015 NPDES Permit renewal process and did a poor job of cutting and pasting to create the current application documents. Such sloppiness is a warning sign about how well Allen Harim will do what it says it will do. That DNREC simply locks those errors into place is a huge red flag about the completeness of the permit review process. The Draft Permit is fundamentally flawed by these failures to comply with the regulations. Instead, a revised permit application and documents should be required, and public comment and a public hearing on the revised documents allowed.

Comment 4. The Proposed Diversion of Noncompliant Wastewater at Allen Harim is Insufficient to Protect Public Health and the Environment.

Precisely because Artesian has no treatment facility of its own, the ability of Artesian to meet its design parameters for the quality of wastewater to be sprayed on its fields depends on the ability of Allen Harim to treat its wastewater to meet the design influent parameters set forth in Artesian's May 2017 Amended DDR. *See* May 5, 2017 Amended DDR at p. 8 Table 3-1 and p. 24 Table 4-1. The lynchpin to ensuring wastewater from Allen Harim complies with the design influent parameters is a system to divert non-compliant wastewater into storage lagoons at Allen Harim so that the water can be re-treated and made compliant. The May 5, 2017 Amended DDR described it this way:

> Wastewater treatment for Phase 1 is being performed in a separate facility by Allen Harim. Sampling will be performed on the Allen Harim Site prior to the pumping to the ANSRWRF storage lagoon to confirm that flow meets the requirements for Unlimited Public Access and the required nitrogen limitations. A 4 million gallon (2-day) storage lagoon will be provided by Allen Harim so that non-conforming effluent can be diverted and retreated prior to being routed to the ANSRWRF facility.

---

instead of Beaverdam Creek, the Allen Harim facility cannot operate in accordance with a pre-Artesian Design Engineer Report. As a result, approval of the operating permit would violate this requirement of the Regulations. Or Allen Harim must construct and operate what the 2015 Design Report requires: a system with much more robust nitrogen removal, which would be more protective of surface and groundwater resources than the system represented in these operating permits. If in fact Allen Harim wants to operate a "send-it-to-ANSRWRF" design, then Allen Harim must submit a new construction permit application, with its new Artesian-based design, and then have that new Design Engineer Report govern its operating permit.

May 5, 2017 Amended DDR at p. 25. At the Artesian construction permit stage in 2017, the details of this automatic diversion were murky; indeed, Artesian punted the issue to the operational permit stage:

> A 4 million gallon (2-day) storage lagoon will be provided by Allen Harim on-site so that non-conforming effluent can be diverted and retreated prior to being routed to the ANSRWRF facility in accordance with [7 Del. Admin. C. 7101 §] 6.3.2.3.2.4.[8] The details regarding how the diversion will be accomplished and which parameters will trigger automatic diversion will be addressed in the amended Allen Harim operations permit.

August 18, 2017 Amended Design Development Report Addendum 1 at p. 7.[9]

The Allen Harim operating permit application now reveals the details of this "automatic diversion." They are found in Section 4.0 of Allen Harim's Operations & Maintenance ("O&M") Plan. O&M Plan p. 50 sets forth the following:

[8] That regulation reads: "Automatic diversion of wastewater that fails to meet the operating criteria must be included in the system design" of a spray irrigation system. That Artesian claimed to satisfy this regulatory requirement for its construction permit by pointing to Allen Harim is further evidence of the linkage between the two systems and the two permits and supports Comment 2 *supra*.

[9] A copy of the August 18, 2017 Amended Design Development Report Addendum 1 is being provided with these comments to assure it is part of the record before the Secretary.

Corrective Measures

A routine compliance sample as defined in Influent and Effluent Monitoring Table that is above the Action Threshold means that Allen Harim is out of compliance with its permit conditions, and must divert flow to its onsite storage lagoon and take corrective measures to return to discharging compliant effluent.

Action Steps: [9]

1. Notify DNREC and Artesian of sample results.
2. Immediately divert flow into Allen Harim offline storage lagoon.
   a. Allen Harim and Artesian will review available Operations data and develop an Action Plan for resuming normal discharge.
      i. As part of this Action Plan Artesian may temporarily cease spray operations to assess the water quality in the ANSRWRF storage lagoon.
3. Allen Harim increases the sampling frequency to daily samples of the type defined in the Influent and Effluent Monitoring Table.
   a. Sampling frequency returns to normal after three consecutive results less than or equal to the Action Threshold.
4. Allen Harim performs troubleshooting and corrects flow to return to compliance.

The draft permit appears to adopt the O&M Plan approach:

> Wastewater that fails to meet the operating criteria as described in the Operation and Maintenance Plan (O&M Plan) including process control testing results of > 30 mg/L for Nitrate as N and total Nitrogen (as verified by laboratory results) shall be automatically diverted into the on-site storage lagoons designated in the O&M Plan.

Special Condition a (page 15 of 17). Thus, diversion happens when a "routine compliance sample" shows some pollutant above an "Action Threshold."

Page 47 of the O&M Plan provides the "sampling protocol which will be used by Allen Harim to maintain compliance with the regulations." The Table setting forth this protocol shows:

Influent & Effluent Monitoring Table 1

Parameter	Unit	Frequency	Sample Type	
			Influent	Effluent
Flow	Gallons Per Day	Continuous	Recorded	Recorded
BOD_5	mg/L	2 x Month	Grab	Composite
TSS	mg/L	2 x Month	Grab	Composite
Total Dissolved Solids	mg/L	Quarterly	N/A	Grab
Fecal Coliform	Col/100 ml	Quarterly	N/A	Grab
Total Nitrogen	mg/L	1 x Week	Grab	Composite
Ammonia Nitrogen	mg/L	Monthly	Grab	Composite
Nitrate/ Nitrite as Nitrogen	mg/L	Monthly	Grab	Composite
pH	S.U.	3 x per Week	Grab	Composite
Total Phosphorus	mg/L	Monthly	Grab	Composite
Chloride	mg/L	Quarterly	Grab	Composite
Turbidity	NTU	Continuous	N/A	

[9]

The Draft Permit narrows the list of "diversion parameters" and changes the sampling types to the following:

Parameter	Unit Measurement	Monitoring Frequency	Sample Type Effluent
*BOD5	mg/L	1 x Week	Grab
COD	mg/L	5 x Week	Grab
Nitrate	mg/L	Daily	Composite & Grab
Total Nitrogen	mg/L	Daily	Composite & Grab
Dissolved Oxygen	mg/L	5 x Week	Grab

[9]

Draft Permit Special Condition a (Page 15 of 17). This sampling protocol reveals five significant problems with the illusion of "automatic diversion" of noncompliant wastewater in Allen Harim's effluent heading to ANSRWRF:

[10]

Problem 1. Some Pollutants Known to be in the Allen Harim Effluent Will Never Be Tested For Compliance with Design Standards. The Table 1 shown here does not list testing frequency for all of the parameters Artesian claimed were design limits in its construction permit application. In addition to Flow, BOD_5, Total Suspended Solids, Turbidity, Fecal Coliform, Total Nitrogen, Ammonia, Nitrate/Nitrite, phosphorus, pH, and Chlorine Residual listed on Table 1 above, Artesian's May 5, 2017 Amended DDR lists design influent characteristics for Lead, Zinc, Copper, Nickel, Cadmium, and Aluminum. *See* May 5, 2017 Amended DDR at 24 Table 4-1. According to Effluent Sampling from Allen Harim reported in Table 4-2, Copper, Nickel, Zinc, and Aluminum were detected in Allen Harim wastewater. *See* May 5, 2017 Amended DDR at 24 Table 4-1. In the case of Zinc, Copper, Nickel, and Aluminum, the Table 4-2 results show measured values ***at or above the design characteristics*** in Table 4-1. In other words, history shows that Allen Harim has exceeded some of the design characteristics. In addition, the Draft Operating Permit for Artesian requires that the sprayed effluent must be monitored for Lead, Zinc, Copper, Nickel, and Cadmium, so clearly those parameters are important to DNREC in terms of what will be sprayed on the Artesian fields. Yet none of these parameters are being monitored for purposes of diversion. Thus, wastewater that is noncompliant with these design parameters would **never** be diverted to Allen Harim's holding ponds but would flow straight to ANSRWRF.[10]

Problem 2. There Are No Action Levels for Four of the Monitored Pollutants. Automatic diversion of noncompliant wastewater is, according to Allen Harim's protocol, only triggered if a sample shows values above the Action Thresholds. However, the O&M Plan only has Action Thresholds for seven of the 11 pollutants being monitored. The four without Action Thresholds are Ammonia Nitrogen, Nitrate/Nitrite as Nitrogen, Total Phosphorus, and Chloride. Thus, under the described Allen Harim O&M Plan protocol, diversion would never be triggered for these four pollutants because they would never exceed their (non-existent) Action Threshold.

The Draft Permit perhaps mitigates this issue somewhat by including language suggesting that "process control test results of > 30 mg/L for Nitrate as N and total Nitrogen (as verified by laboratory

---

[10] A similar problem exists on the Artesian side of this arrangement. While the Permit requires sampling of spray field effluent for ten pollutant parameters plus flow, *see* Draft Permit Part II A. Monitoring Requirements 2. Spray Effluent Monitoring Requirements (page 15 of 34), there appears to be no permit limits for many of them. The Artesian Draft Permit, in Part I C. Sprayed Effluent Limitations (page 9 of 34), imposes limits on the pH, Total Residual Chlorine, Chloride and Sodium, but specifically states for each of these that "[t]he point of compliance shall be at Allen Harim's effluent pump station." *Id.* at ¶¶ 6 – 9. There appears to be no requirement in the Allen Harim permit to sample for Sodium, so how that can be achieved is unclear. Artesian's Draft Permit also imposes limits on BOD5, Fecal Coliform, Total Suspended Solids, and Turbidity as part of the "Unlimited Public Access term. *See Id.* at ¶ 14 (page 10 – 11 of 34). However, there appear to be no limits on Ammonia Nitrogen, Cadmium, Copper, Lead, Nickel, Nitrate + Nitrite Nitrogen, and Zinc anywhere in the Permit.

results) shall be automatically diverted . . . ," but that does not cover Total Phosphorus and Chloride. Given the enormous emphasis on nitrogen and phosphorus in the regulations governing spray irrigation, this is an enormous hole in the plan to spray supposedly "clean" water on Artesian's fields.

Even worse is the fact that the Draft Permit's reduced list of "diversion parameters" contains two—COD and Dissolved Oxygen—for which there are no Action Thresholds in the O&M Plan. In other words, DNREC has identified two parameters that are supposed to trigger "diversion," but there is no standard for those parameters which would ever cause actual diversion of wastewater. It creates the illusion of diversion without any actual diversion taking place. That, of course, means that wastewater contaminated with parameters that are supposed to be diverted will in fact flow to ANSRWRF.

Problem 3. There is confusion and a potential conflict over how testing for diversion should be done. The Allen Harim Draft Permit contains a cryptic reference that "the permittee shall sample the effluent for the following diversion parameters using field tests and other Department approved methods." Draft Permit Special Condition a (page 15 of 17). The Draft permit does not specify what "field tests" are or what "other approved Department methods" might be. The failure to specify these testing methods is confusing, as it does not provide either the permittee or the public any guidance as to whether samples will be taken and analyzed in a manner that is appropriate. Further, Part I Section H (Draft Permit page 8 of 17) specifies that "test procedures for the analysis of pollutants shall conform to the applicable test procedures identified in 40 C.F.R. Part 136 or the most recently adopted copy of Standard Methods unless otherwise specified in this permit." It is unclear whether this limits the sampling and analysis for diversion purposes, or whether the "field tests and other Department approved methods" are an example of "unless otherwise specified in this permit" so that the 40 C.F.R. Part 136 and Standard Methods do not apply. The confusion and potential conflict with standard procedures is a result of the failure of the permit drafters to be specific.

Problem 4. The Time Inherent In Sampling and Analyzing Wastewater means Noncompliant Wastewater* Will *Flow to ANSRWRF. The Monitoring Protocol of the O&M Plan, as modified by the Draft Permit, requires that Nitrate as N and total be monitored via Composite Samples. According to the Allen Harim O&M Plan (at p. 45), a composite sample is "[a] combination of individual samples taken at selected time intervals, for some specified time period, to minimize the effect of variability of the individual sample . . .It is required that we sample our effluent for the parameters noted in the NPDES permit. Most of the sampling requirements are based on a composite sample taken over a 24-hour period." Thus, a composite sample being checked for compliance needs 24 hours to be collected; in the meantime, the wastewater is flowing to ANSRWRF. Only after the sample shows the wastewater is noncompliant could automatic diversion kick in. By then, the actual water sampled is past the compliance point—meaning that noncompliant wastewater (which, over a 24-hour period, would be 1.5 – 2.0 Million gallons) cannot be diverted and is already on its way to (if not already arrived at) ANSRWRF.

An additional time factor is that the sample must be analyzed. While Allen Harim plans on having an onsite lab that can test for some parameters, such onsite tests take time—while the wastewater keeps flowing to ANSRWRF because a noncompliant sample result has not yet been detected. *See* O&M Plan at 44. The Plan goes on to state "tests for NPDES permit requirements will be done on a contractual basis using a testing laboratory. *Id.* That means that the samples must be sent offsite and lab results produced before diversion can occur—all while the wastewater keeps flowing to ANSRWRF because a noncompliant sample result has not yet been detected. Further, some of the tests take time to perform. For example, the "5" in BOD_5 represents the number of days of incubation before the result is generated. Thus, a sample showing noncompliance for BOD_5 would allow *at least* 5 days of potentially noncompliant wastewater (7.5 – 10.0 Million gallons) to flow to ANSRWRF just during the lab analysis time before diversion would occur.

Quite simply, diversion of wastewater found to be noncompliant would not be immediate—meaning that ANSRWRF will receive noncompliant wastewater. And because ANSRWRF does not have the ability to treat the wastewater beyond chlorination, that noncompliant wastewater would be sprayed on the spray fields in contravention of the story Artesian has been telling since the construction permit proceedings. Nothing in the application materials suggests that this problem can or will be avoided.

Although the focus here is on sampling at the Allen Harim side of things, it is important to note that the Artesian Draft Permit creates a similar problem. That Permit requires that sprayed effluent be sampled "from a sampling port located at the discharge side of the irrigation pumps." Draft Permit Part II A. Monitoring Requirements 2. Sprayed Effluent Monitoring Requirements (page 15 of 34). Eight of the ten pollutant parameters (Ammonia Nitrogen, Cadmium, Copper, Lead, Nickel, Nitrate + Nitrite Nitrogen, Total Nitrogen, and Zinc) must be collected as Composite Samples. Here, timing is almost irrelevant: no matter what the sample shows (i.e., no matter how high the concentration of pollutant in the spray effluent might be), it is too late because the water will have already been sprayed on the fields before a sample could be taken and analyzed. Further, the sampling frequency (Total Nitrogen 2x a month, Ammonia Nitrogen and Nitrate + Nitrite Nitrogen monthly, and the remainder annually) means that significant periods of time between sample events will take place so that significant volumes of high pollutant water could be sprayed on the fields. That by itself is unacceptable risk.

Problem 5. The Surrogate Testing Parameters Do Not Solve These Problems. The O&M Plan for Allen Harim suggests that "surrogate" parameters of Chemical Oxygen Demand (COD) and Nitrate can be tested by the on-site lab "in order to provide an early indicator of potential exceedances of BOD_5 and Total Nitrogen." O&M Plan at p. 49. This approach is inadequate for several reasons. First, at best the sampling provides additional monitoring only for 2 of the 11 pollutants listed on the monitoring table and the 16 pollutants identified in the May 2017 Amended DDR Design parameters. This means that most of the parameters of concern will not receive this additional coverage, and so it cannot address the gaps in coverage noted above in the earlier problems described above. Second, the protocol outlined on p. 49 of the O&M Plan shows that, if the once-a-day surrogate grab samples is above the established limit, diversion does not occur; rather, additional grab samples are to be taken over another 24-hour period. If those suggest possible noncompliance for BOD_5 or Total Nitrogen, *then* a composite sample must be taken. Thus, at least 48 hours of sampling (24 hours for additional grab samples, 24 hours for the composite sample) must take place—meaning 3 Million Gallons of suspected noncompliant wastewater will flow to ANSRWRF. Then the time for formal analysis of the composite sample by the outside lab must pass—which will be at least 5 days for the BOD_5 sample—so that anywhere from 7.5 to 10.0 Million *additional* gallons of noncompliant wastewater will flow before the formal determination of the need for diversion occurs.

The Draft Permit does not solve this problem. It does not specify when diversion must occur, but defaults to a failure to meet the operating criteria as described in the O&M Plan. Draft Permit Special Condition a (page 15 of 17).

Because of all these problems, the "diversion" of all noncompliant wastewater at Allen Harim is an illusion. Significant amounts of noncompliant wastewater can and will flow to ANSRWRF under the proposal set forth in these applications and be sprayed on Artesian's fields. As a result, the operations plan in these documents does not meet the protection promised at the Artesian construction permit stage, and thus the requested operations permits should not be granted.

Comment 5. Allen Harim Will Have Capacity Problems With Diverted Wastewater Given Its Operational Plan For Monitoring.

Allen Harim proposes that automatic diversion will result in diverted water being handled in the following way:

> The following sequential diversion of non-compliant effluent will occur when WWTP effluent exceeds the above action limits.. The first 2.0 million gallons of flow would go to the old storm water lagoon. [11] The next 2.0 million gallons will go to the anoxic ponds. If the diversion exceeds 4.0 million gallons, the additional flow will be diverted to the old anaerobic lagoon. Diversion to the old anaerobic lagoon will not occur unless it is absolutely required. The old anaerobic lagoon will be in the process of cleaning with a new liner installed. Synagro has agreed to accept diversion water during the clean out process (see appendix 5).

O&M Plan, p. 50. The problem with this approach is that if a diversion occurs, it is almost guaranteed that Allen Harim will have to put diverted wastewater into old anaerobic lagoon that it says will not occur. The reason is that Allen Harim's protocol for when a noncompliant sample comes back, set forth in the Corrective Measures outlined on O&M Plan p. 50, mandates that Allen Harim increase sampling to daily and keep sampling daily until three consecutive samples show compliance. Presumably, water must be diverted to the lagoons and ponds until the 3 consecutive samples show compliance.[11] That

[11] If it does not mean that wastewater will be diverted until the 3 consecutive samples show compliance, then what this means is that wastewater—already found noncompliant by the sample triggering diversion—is being sent to ANSRWRF without any assurance that it is in compliance. This would further undermine (if not completely puncture) the illusion of no noncompliant wastewater going to ANSRWRF.

would mean at least 3 days, or 4.5 Million Gallons, of diversion (with the possibility of at least 8 days, or 12 Million Gallons, if the parameter is BOD_5). Under any of these scenarios, at least some of the water will have to flow to the old anaerobic lagoon—perhaps a significant amount.

It is not at all clear how flow to the old anaerobic lagoon can occur during the mandated cleanout of the lagoon. Draft Permit Part I Paragraph M Schedule of Compliance sub-paragraph a (page 9-10 of 17) requires the cleanout of the old lagoon by July 1, 2021. In other words, cleanout will be happening for nearly two years after issuance of the draft permit. How flow to the lagoon can occur and how it will be handled during the cleanout is not spelled out in either the Draft Permit or the O&M Plan. This is important because flow into the lagoon during the cleanout period raises the potential for contaminants in the old lagoon to enter the Allen Harim wastewater treatment system when that water is pumped back for re-treatment. Nothing in any of the papers submitted thus far indicate what those parameters are or whether the treatment system could handle them.

Upon re-establishing compliance, the water in the ponds must be treated along with the wastewater generated by the process that day. Because there appears to be no requirement that Allen Harim scale back its operations while water in the ponds is re-treated, it may take a significant amount of time to work off the water in the ponds. Of course, if another sample shows noncompliance, then the water backup only worsens. The O&M Plan does not explain how Allen Harim would recover in the case of a diversion. Without specific provisions governing this, the proposal will be unworkable.

Comment 6. The "Unlimited Public Access" Standard Does Not Prove That The Wastewater Sprayed On Artesian Fields Is Safe. [12]

Artesian has long touted the fact that it will require Allen Harim to treat its wastewater to satisfy the "Unlimited Public Access" standards under the regulations, as if that indicates that the water will be clean and safe. Disturbingly, DNREC appears to adopt this line, stating in the Public Hearing announcement in its website that "The effluent will receive a high level of treatment to meet the "Unlimited Public Access" requirement at the Allen Harim Wastewater Treatment Plant." There is much less to this claim than meets the eye.

The unlimited public access standards are found at 7 Del. Admin. C. 7101 § 6.3.2.3.3.2. According to this section, the standard is designed for sites that are "landscaped areas such as golf courses, residential lawns, cemeteries, parks, and highway medians which may not have adequate buffer zones and are accessible to the public at all times"—in other words, where people can be found walking in the areas sprayed. The standard only requires treatment to certain average concentrations for four pollutants: BOD_5, Fecal Coliform, Total Suspended Solids, and Turbidity. It does not require treatment to any levels for contaminants that can impact groundwater, such as nitrogen, ammonia, phosphorus, or any of the metals or other contaminants listed in the Design Criteria of Artesian's May 5, 2017 Amended DDR. Thus, while it may protect persons walking on the spray fields from acute problems caused by exposure to these four pollutants, treatment to "Unlimited Public Access" tells DNREC nothing about long-term effects on soil and groundwater resources. It is a meaningless standard to measure against for any environmental issue beyond direct surface exposure. It therefore should not be used as some kind of "proof" of the "cleanliness" or "environmental friendliness" of the wastewater generated by Allen Harim.

Comment 7. The Artesian Operating Permit Must Regulate Impacts Caused By Contamination Moved Via Spray-Induced Groundwater Additions. [13]

Artesian's Field G—the first field Artesian intends to spray on after operations commence—is directly across the street and upgradient from the spray fields used by Clean Delaware. As DNREC well knows, Clean Delaware is subject to enforcement actions by DNREC, and have been required to sample the groundwater in its fields. An August 2017 Quarterly report from Clean Delaware (a copy of which is submitted with the physical copy of these comments) shows that the groundwater in those fields is contaminated with high levels of several pollutants.[12] Christopher Grobbell, Appellant's Expert in the EAB No. 2017-14 proceeding, has analyzed the Clean Delaware data and found not only that the groundwater under the Clean Delaware site is contaminated, but also that the prevalent groundwater flow direction means that the Clean Delaware contamination is headed towards residences located downgradient from the Clean Delaware site. Mr. Grobbel has also determined that Artesian's spraying hundreds of millions of gallons of water on Field G will accelerate that movement of contaminants in the residential area, which rely upon the groundwater resources for drinking water. *See* Letter of Christopher Grobbel attached to these comments.[13]

7 Del. Admin. C. 7101 § 6.5.3.2.3 empowers DNREC to establish specific permit conditions for "the protection of the environment and the public health." The characteristics that can inform such conditions include "size of the site and its proximity to population centers, ground and surface water" (6.5.3.2.3.3), and "potential for adverse environmental impacts to groundwater resources or surface water bodies" (6.5.3.2.3.7). DNREC must protect these residences and other potential drinking water uses downgradient from Field G from these known consequences of Artesian spraying on Field G.

Comment 8. The Artesian Draft Permit Allows Spraying That Will Exceed The Limits For Nitrogen Concentrations in Groundwater.

Artesian's Construction Permit documents describe a spray irrigation system design in which the nitrogen concentration being contributed to groundwater under the spray field—after all crop take up and other nitrogen eliminating factors allegedly occurring in a spray field—is 9.9 mg/L. *See* May 5, 2017 Amended Design Development Report Appendix G (and echoed in Artesian July 2019 O&M Plan Appendix C. Note that this 9.9 mg/l design limit exists *for each month*. This is literally 0.1 mg/L under

[12] We have sought more recent Clean Delaware data from DNREC via FOIA, but were prevented from seeing it because DNREC claimed a pending litigation/investigation exception under FOIA. DNREC, however, can review the records for itself (which would then make them part of the record before the Secretary).

[13] Mr. Grobbel's letter was separately submitted and is already in the record. It is included with physical copy of these comments (and therefore entered into the record again) for ease of reference.

the generally accepted regulatory limit of 10 mg/L. To achieve this 9.9 mg/L design rate, the May 2017 Amended DDR assumes that the Total Nitrogen in the spray effluent does not exceed 30 mg/L.

Artesian's Draft Operating Permit does not impose a Total Nitrogen limit of 30 mg/L in order to achieve this razor-thin level of compliant performance. Instead, it states the following:

> The facility has been designed for an effluent Total Nitrogen concentration of 30 mg/L [May 5, 2017 Amended Design Development Report ANSRWRF Phase I].
>
> If the effluent Total Nitrogen concentration exceeds 37.5 mg/L [Design Value + 25%] in any calendar month, the permittee shall resample the wastewater and submit the additional analyses to the Groundwater Discharges Section. If the effluent Total Nitrogen concentration exceeds 37.5 mg/L for over a three month period, the permittee must have the system evaluated to determine the cause and submit a revised Design Engineer Report to the Groundwater Discharges Section. If the effluent exceeds 45.0 mg/L [Design Value +50%], the Department may invoke the provisions of Part V.A.1 of this permit. Also reference Part II.B.1.

Draft Permit Part I C. Spray Effluent Limitations ¶ 10 (page 10 of 34). In other words, Artesian can exceed the design limit of 30 mg/L at any concentration for one or two months without any consequence. No action is triggered unless there are three months of Design Value + 25%--meaning that concentrations greater than 30 mg/L but less than 37 mg/l will not trigger any compliance action. Only if there are 3 months of 37.5 mg/l is there any consequence—and the consequence is not a stoppage but simply more engineering over an unspecified period. If the concentration is Design + 50%, the Department "may invoke" the provision of Part V.A.1 (commencement of the process of revoking the permit), but there is no guarantee that any such revocation procedure will in fact take place. In the interim, every 0.1 mg/l of total nitrogen above 30 mg/l means that Artesian exceeds the design criteria (as would be the 10 mg/l regulatory standard). In short, the Draft Permit lacks meaningful constraints to assure that the 30 mg/L spray effluent concentration—necessary to generate the 9.9 mg/L design criteria—will in fact occur.

Comment 9. The Total Nitrogen limits in the Artesian Draft Permit Conflict with Other Provisions of the Permit and Artesian's O&M Plan.

Perhaps as a reaction to the problem posed by the (non)limits on Total Nitrogen concentrations, the Artesian Draft Permit also includes what it calls "the total amount of nitrogen that may be applied to each field" calculated on a lbs/acre-year basis:

11. The total amount of nitrogen that may be applied to each spray field acre shall not exceed the following. This amount includes supplemental fertilizers, the nitrogen supplied from the effluent, and any other source. [Taken from 20190716 Active Spreadsheet Nitrogen Balance]

Crop Type	**Nitrogen Loading Limit (lbs/acre-year)**
Cover – Corn - Barley	334.5
Barley – Soybean – Cover	388.8
Woods (Loblolly Pines)	435.4

Adjustments and reductions for denitrification, ammonia volatilization, evapotranspiration and plant uptake are ***not*** to be factored into the annual reporting of Total Nitrogen Loading for demonstration of compliance with this limit.

Draft Permit Part I C. Spray Effluent Limitations ¶ 11 (page 10 of 34). The problem here is that the ¶ 11 Total Nitrogen Annual Limits conflict with another provision of the Draft Permit.

Paragraph 1 of this same Spray Effluent Limitations section of the Permit requires that Artesian's facility "shall be operated in accordance with the Nitrogen Balance provided in Appendix C of the July 2019 *Operation and Maintenance Plan* for ANSRWRF." Draft Permit Part I C. Spray Effluent Limitations ¶ 1 (page 8 of 34). As a result, the Permit requires Artesian to follow what the Nitrogen Balance spreadsheets in Appendix C say.

The Nitrogen Balance spreadsheet referenced in this provision supplies a detailed calculation of the amount of nitrogen coming into the Spray Fields. Given that the annual limit in ¶ 11 (page 10 of 34) expressly excludes taking credit for crop uptake and other "reductions" of nitrogen, it appears that the most relevant line on the Spreadsheets for each field is Line 22 Total Nitrogen Applied. This line shows lbs/acre of nitrogen on a monthly basis before any reductions, with an annual number shown in the SUM column. Note also that the spreadsheets posit a two-year cycle of planting.

The Line 22 SUM values for the fields covered by Permit show the following lbs/acre-year of Total Nitrogen:

	Year 1	Year 2
Field D Crop w/o Pivot D4	339.4	469.4
Field D Crop w/ Pivot D4	339.5	469.4
Field E Crop	339.5	469.4
Field G Crop	339.5	469.4

The problem is that all four fields would in Year 1 exceed the 334.5 lbs/acre annual limit in ¶ 11 for Cover-Corn-Barley (even though the Cover-Corn-Barley planting mixture is what is used in the Year 1 calculations, *see* Line 29 in each Spreadsheet). In Year 2 all four fields would far exceed both the 334.5 lbs/acre annual limit Cover-Corn-Barley and the 388.8 lbs/acre annual limit for Barley-Soybean-Cover (even though the Barley-Soybean-Cover is the planting mixture used in Year 2, *see* Line 29 of the Spreadsheets). Even averaging the numbers (which ¶ 11's imposition of annual limits would seem to exclude) would not bring the amounts into compliance with ¶ 11's annual limits. Thus, the Permit creates a fundamental contradiction: follow the Nitrogen Balance in Appendix C and thereby violate the annual limits, or follow the annual limits but violate the requirement to follow the Nitrogen Balance in Appendix C. Artesian cannot comply with both. The solution should be to remove or modify the ¶ 1 requirement of compliance with the O&M Plan Appendix C Nitrogen Balance so that the Permit allows the lower amount of nitrogen to be applied (though that would still be too much nitrogen for this area).

Thank you for the opportunity to submit this set of public comments.

Sincerely,

Exhibits to these Public Comments (included in hard copy being sent in)
1 – May 22, 2018 Hearing Transcript in EAB No. 2017-14
2 – March 12, 2019 Hearing Transcript in EAB No. 2017-14
3 – May 5, 2017 Amended Design Development Report
4 – January 27, 2017 Wastewater Services Agreement between Artesian and Allen Harim
5 – August 18, 2017 Amended Design Development Report Addendum 1
6 – Clean Delaware August 2017 Quarterly Report
7 – August 19, 2019 Letter from Christopher Grobbel

ANOTATIONS FOR APPENDIX TAB 2

[1] Addressed to the person identified in Public Notice and who sat as Hearing Officer at Public Hearing

[2] Identifies the Proceeding. In this case (like in Public Comment in Appendix Tab 1), DNREC had created a Docket for the permit proceeding, and so the Docket # is used

[3] Set up as a series of Public Comments submitted in a single document. Structure is to give a summary statement of what the comment is about, then beneath the summary a detailed statement setting out the full comments.

[4] Citing to specific regulatory requirements as basis of comment (remember, DNREC is required to follow the law, and regulatory requirements are the law in these situations)

[5] Reference to and attachment of certain documents to make sure they are in the record before the Secretary in case of an appeal

[6] Using specific quotations from cited and attached document to support particular assertions.

[7] Describing the regulatory requirement and then (in next ¶s) showing how the regulatory requirement was not met. Note that additional facts and arguments are included in footnotes

[8] Uses statements in application and other documents (¶s above) to compare/contrast with provisions of the draft permit (in ¶s below)

[9] Literally cut and pasted from the draft permit pdf file.

[10] First in a series of problems that the draft permit language creates. Comment walks through the consequences of the permit provisions pasted above

[11] Cut and pasted from a permit application pdf file

[12] Comment based on the limited nature of the regulatory requirements

[13] Additional argument based on consequences of facility operation that should be (but have not yet been) considered in preparation of draft permit

APPENDIX TAB 3

Annotations on Sheet following the Standing Declaration Document

BEFORE THE ENVIRONMENTAL APPEALS BOARD
OF THE STATE OF DELAWARE

Food & Water Watch,	)	
	)	
Appellant	)	
	)	**EAB Appeal No. 2015-09** [1]
v.	)	
	)	Declaration of Maria Payan
Secretary David Smalls, Delaware Department of Natural Resources and Environmental Control,	)	
	)	
Appellee	)	
	)	

DECLARATION OF MARIA PAYAN [2]

I, Maria Payan, do hereby declare:

1. My name is Maria Payan, and I reside at [redacted], [redacted]. I have lived there since October 2015. Unless otherwise stated, I have personal knowledge of all of the facts stated below. [3]

2. I have been a member of Food & Water Watch for approximately the past two years. I make this declaration in support of Food & Water Watch's appeal of Delaware's general permit for broiler chicken concentrated animal feeding operations ("CAFOs") that do not land apply waste.

3. I am also a consultant with the Socially Responsible Agricultural Project ("SRAP"), and have held this position since October 2010. As a consultant with SRAP, I am responsible for working with rural communities directly impacted by water and air pollution from CAFOs. This work includes supporting communities in fighting new CAFO construction and expansion throughout Delaware, as well as in Maryland, Pennsylvania, and New York. I regularly meet with rural citizens and community organizations to provide information and training, including training on how CAFOs are regulated in different states and how to conduct citizen water quality monitoring to detect CAFO pollution. I [4]
routinely assist communities in commenting on CAFO regulations and permits and making requests for public hearings on CAFO issues. I have also invested significant time and resources in investigating potential pollution at CAFOs, including by participating in flyovers of broiler chicken CAFOs and conducting water monitoring at CAFOs of concern to rural citizens.

4. I am aware that nitrogen, phosphorus, and pathogen pollution has impaired water quality in many of Delaware's rivers and streams, and I regularly see signs in various Delaware locations warning that swimming or fishing in local waterways is not safe. I am also aware that the Chesapeake Bay is impaired by nutrient pollution and is now subject to a Bay-wide cleanup plan for nutrient and sediment pollution.

5. I believe that CAFOs are contributing nitrogen, phosphorus, and pathogen pollution to waterways throughout Delaware, because I have personally observed ditches leading directly off of broiler CAFO facilities. I have noticed that such ditches leading from or near CAFOs frequently smell like animal waste and contain visible algae. Based on my observations, it seems typical of Delaware broiler CAFOs to have ditches running out from their facilities, though it is not always possible to see these aspects of CAFOs from the public road.

6. I have trained members of several community organizations to monitor water quality at public access points up- and down-stream of CAFO operations, including broiler, layer, and hog operations. As far as I know, three of these groups are still conducting regular citizen monitoring for the purpose of identifying any illegal CAFO discharges.

7. I have plans to imminently begin conducting my own water quality monitoring near a Delaware broiler chicken CAFO. I recently requested a public [5]
hearing related to this facility, and intend to collect water quality data due to my concerns that the facility's lack of adequate manure storage facilities and other means to prevent runoff will lead to pollution discharges and degrade downstream waterways. I believe this monitoring is necessary to demonstrate that Delaware must impose stronger requirements on this facility to protect water quality. I will

base my surface water monitoring on past CAFO monitoring I have done and trainings I have received.

8. Designing and implementing this monitoring plan will require a significant personal investment of time and financial resources. I intend to purchase test strips that measure nitrate, ammonia, and pH, and will need to drive more than an hour each way to conduct each round of monitoring. If any sample results indicate pollution levels of concern, I will need to collect "grab" samples of water to send to a certified lab, which will be able to confirm my results. The estimated cost of supplies for monitoring this single facility could reach as much as $100.00.

9. Based on my past monitoring experience, I estimate that using maps, online resources, and in-person observations, it will take several hours to identify monitoring locations at public access points up- and downstream of the facility. To collect dry weather "baseline" water quality data and establish a pattern of water quality data from wet weather events, I will need to adjust my schedule to accommodate numerous several-hour trips to conduct representative monitoring at these locations over the next several months. If Delaware required this CAFO to conduct its own representative surface water monitoring, I would not feel the need to spend my time and money to document whether the facility is in compliance with anti-pollution laws and regulations.

10. My concerns about broiler CAFO pollution in Delaware have also affected my recreational activities in several ways. I grew up in the region and [6] have regularly visited Delaware's and Maryland's beaches since I was twelve years old. My first job was on the boardwalk. Until recently, I would regularly swim in the ocean, crab off of the docks, fish, and eat the crabs and fish I caught. Bethany State Park is only about twenty minutes from my house, and I am also close to Prime Hook State Park, and I would visit them often if I felt it was safe. But because of my knowledge of CAFO water pollution and the threats it poses to public health, I will no longer swim in these beaches or eat locally caught fish or crabs. I planned to visit Prime Hook State Park this year on Memorial Day, but changed my plans when the state closed the park's beaches due to *Enteroccocus* bacteria, a pathogen associated with livestock and human waste. I am aware that some *Enteroccocus* infections can be difficult to treat, due to increasing resistance to certain antibiotics. I have not even visited the beach once this year because my fear of the polluted water makes visiting the beach unenjoyable.

11. My awareness of and concerns about pollution from broiler CAFOs also make it much less enjoyable for me when I recreate near rivers and streams throughout the state. For example, I frequently visit friends who live on the Indian River, and am concerned that the numerous CAFOs in the area have degraded the waterway and made it unsafe for boating or swimming. This concern has severely

diminished my enjoyment of these visits, and I am not willing to swim or walk in the water or eat fish caught in it.

12. By refusing to require Delaware broiler CAFOs to monitor their own discharges for common poultry litter pollutants, DNREC makes it necessary for me to spend my time and resources, as well as SRAP's resources, conducting [7] additional water quality monitoring and training citizens to conduct water quality monitoring to protect their own health and safety. It also limits my and other Delaware residents' access to information about the safety of our public waterways. For these reasons, the agency's actions serve to heighten my fears and concerns, and decrease my enjoyment of my local waterways. Access to information about CAFO pollution and whether Delaware CAFOs meet the requirements in the broiler CAFO permit is vital to my work to help protect rural communities and restore local waterways. The lack of this monitoring information has also made me feel it is necessary to avoid swimming and other recreation that involves direct contact with waterways, has kept me from fishing and crabbing as I used to, and has made recreation near Delaware's beaches, rivers, and streams less enjoyable due to my knowledge of agricultural pollution's degradation of these resources.

I declare under penalty of perjury that the foregoing is true and correct.

Executed on July 29, 2016.

Maria Payan

Maria Payan

DECLARATION OF MARTIN LAMPNER [8]

I, Martin Lampner, do hereby declare, under penalty of perjury, that if called I would testify as follows:

1. I am one of the Appellants in *Martin Lampner et al. v. Delaware Dept. of Natural Resources and Environmental Control*, No. 2019-02, currently pending before the [9]
Environmental Appeals Board. I have personal knowledge of the matters set forth herein.

2. I currently reside at [redacted] ([redacted]). My wife and I have owned this home for seven years, and have been full-time residents for the past 3 years. We have access to and regularly use the Whites Creek Marina boat ramp and [10]
walkways. I regularly kayak on the Creek, and had a small dinghy sailboat I sailed out of the Marina. I anticipate purchasing a new boat within the next 12 months and am planning to dock at Whites Creek Marina.

3. The building of the TAC Beacon marina as envisioned by the plan approved in the Secretary's Order will disrupt and diminish my recreational enjoyment of Whites Creek. In particular: [11]

> A. The channel from the Marina to Whites Creek is very narrow and shallow. The TAC Beacon proposed marina is located in a S bend in the Creek with limited sight lines and tall grasses in an adjoining protected marsh across the Creek. The TAC Beacon marina (with its boat ramp) will increase congestion in the Creek at its narrowest section as well as an area with numerous blind spots. This will make navigation more difficult and riskier for me and increase the risk of groundings or collisions and property damage. This will be even more pronounced at high tides, as the Creek near the proposed marina is difficult if not impossible to navigate at low tide, and so traffic tends to concentrate during higher tide periods. As a result, it will be less enjoyable to boat on the Creek.
>
> B. The proposed Boat Ramp, as well as the new TAC Beacon dock, will further narrow the area for boats to pass by safely, and thereby adversely impact navigation. Currently, the shallows TAC Beacon proposes to use for its dockage provide the path with the best visibility and furthest from the channel used by power craft. Because the channel is so narrow, proper nautical passage in the Creek, already challenging at low tide such as passing a boat travelling in the opposite direction is very precarious and will be so for more of the day.
>
> C. The decision to encourage jet skis in the creek, by providing jet ski pads for their storage and docking will also make this water less attractive to a kayaker. Jet Skis on plane to not tend to throw much of a wake but in the narrow congested area this facility will be built in they will not be able to attain the speed needed to get up on plane and therefore will throw a wake. Particularly in narrow waters wakes pose a threat to kayak users. The constriction of the area with the docks and vessels coming and going from them will also make it harder to turn the kayak to take the wave on its bow rather than broadside. As such the likelihood of discomfort or being capsized increases.

D. The boat and jet ski traffic and the floating dock contemplated at the TAB Beacon marina will disturb the bottom of the Creek, stirring up excess nutrients trapped in the sediment (thereby polluting the water in the Creek) and causing sediment to silt in the channel. This will adversely impact fish, crabs, and other aquatic wildlife. This reduces the pleasure that comes from viewing marine life in the relative clarity of the water in its current state.

E. In connection with the building of the TAC Beacon marina, significant amounts of trees and other shoreline barrier vegetation have been removed from the area. This has resulted in an increase in sediment flowing into the Creek and further restrict proper passage of boats to and from Whites Creek Marina.

As a result of all these changes, my enjoyment of boating and recreating on Whites Creek has already been, and will continue to be, diminished as a result of the TAC Beacon marina project. Dependent on the type of boat I purchase in the future I may need to also consider docking or launching from facilities not impacted by the project as completion may further limit the types of vessels I can consider that could safely traverse the area.

4. I am also concerned that the increased boat traffic and decreased enjoyment of Whites Creek will decrease the property value of my home. [12]

5. I was very concerned about the potential effects of the TAC Beacon project, and so monitored the proceedings leading up to the Secretary's Order approving the project. I spoke at the public hearing on TAC Beacon's original application. I also have been quoted in the local media and more recently have had letters published as well. At no time was I made aware—by DNREC or by TAC Beacon—that a significantly different design had been submitted to DNREC. This was learned of after the public hearing and public comment has closed. Had I known of the amended permit application by TAC Beacon, I would have wanted to submit further comments. I repeatedly contacted the department via e-mail and phone during the months of July, August and September 2017 to follow up on a commitment that the report of the hearing officer would be published prior to any action. In September 2017 I was informed that the plan had been amended and addressed our concerns. It did not and no public notice of the amended file was published. I had to ask repeatedly for the amended proposal. When it was finally received I was informed there would be no further comment, that the only option would be an Appeal if and when the Secretary approved the project.

I declare under penalty of perjury under the laws of Delaware that the foregoing is true and correct.

Executed: May 10, 2019

Martin Lampner

ANOTATIONS FOR APPENDIX TAB 3

Payan Declaration

[1] Example of an appeal/case caption

[2] Title: "Declaration of [Declarant's Name]"

[3] As shown in caption above, Appellant is an organization, so standing must be established through members of the organization. This ¶ establishes membership of the Declarant

[4] Establishing personal knowledge of the Declarant (next several ¶)

[5] Establishing personal involvement that will result in economic injury/expense

[6] Establishing injury to recreational interests because activities are less enjoyable or no longer done

[7] Summary Statement of the injuries

Lampner Declaration

[8] Version of a Declaration without a case caption

[9] Statement of personal knowledge of facts in the Declaration

[10] Establishes recreational interest

[11] Description of how the project will injure the previously identified recreational interest

[12] Statement to establish possible economic injury

APPENDIX TAB 4

Annotations on Sheet following the Statement of Appeal Document

Widener University
Delaware Law School

Environmental & Natural Resources Law Clinic
Kenneth T. Kristl, Esq., Director

April 5, 2019

VIA EMAIL AND OVERNIGHT DELIVERY

Environmental Appeals Board
89 Kings Highway [1]
Dover, DE 19901
Attn: Administrative Assistant to the Environmental Appeals Board

RE: Statement of Appeal to the Environmental Appeals Board for Secretary's Order No. 2019-W-0015, Approving a Marina Permit and Subaqueous Lands Lease for TAC Beacon 1, LLC to construct and operate a minor marina at The Solitudes of White Creek Community, Ocean View, Sussex County, Delaware [2]

Pursuant to 7 Del. C. §§ 6008 and 7210, Martin Lampner and the 98 other individuals listed on the List of Appellants attached hereto (collectively, "Appellants") submit this written statement of appeal to the Delaware Environmental Appeals Board. Appellants challenge the Secretary of Delaware Department of Natural Resources and Environmental Control's ("Department" or "DNREC") Order No. 2019-W-0015 ("Secretary's Order"), dated March 5, 2019 but not publicly noticed until March 20, 2019. The Secretary's Order approves a Marina Permit and Subaqueous Lands Lease for TAC Beacon 1, LLC to construct and operate a minor marina at The Solitudes of White Creek Community, Ocean View, Sussex County, Delaware. A fifty dollar ($50.00) deposit for costs accompanies this Statement of Appeal. [3]

The Appellants in this appeal are represented by Kenneth T. Kristl, Esq. and the Environmental and Natural Resources Law Clinic (Clinic), located at the Widener University Delaware Law School in Wilmington, DE. The Clinic provides representation and legal assistance to public interest organizations and individuals on environmental matters in Delaware and other Mid-Atlantic states.

I. Interests That Have Been Substantially Affected [4]

Appellants are individuals who recreate (via boating, kayaking, bird watching, and other recreational activities) and/or own boat slips or docks on White Creek in and near the location of the marina approved by the Secretary's Order. Each of the Appellant's recreational, aesthetic, and/or property interests and the enjoyment of the same will be adversely affected and diminished by the proposed marina approved by the Secretary's Order. As such, each Appellant is a "person whose interest is substantially affected by" an "action of the Secretary," and is therefore entitled to bring this appeal under 7 Del. C. §§ 6008(a) and 7210.

Widener University Delaware Law School, 4601 Concord Pike, Wilmington, DE 19803-0406
t: 302-477-2053 f: 302-477-2032 e: ktkristl@widener.edu delawarelaw.widener.edu

II. Allegation That The Secretary's Order Was Improperly Issued [5]

The Secretary, in issuing the Order, has acted arbitrarily, capriciously, and contrary to law in that:

a. The issuance of the Secretary's Order, and the approvals contained therein, were done without compliance with the applicable statutory and regulatory provisions requiring public notice and comment after submission of an application;

b. The issuance of the Secretary's Order, and the approvals contained therein, were done without compliance with the applicable statutory and regulatory provisions governing leases of subaqueous lands; and

c. The issuance of the Secretary's Order, and the approvals contained therein, were done without compliance with the applicable statutory and regulatory provisions governing marinas.

III. Reasons Why The Secretary's Order Was Improperly Issued [6]

The Secretary's Order is arbitrary, capricious, and/or contrary to law for numerous reasons.

A. The Secretary's Order, and the Approvals contained therein, Were Issued Without Compliance with Applicable Statutory and Regulatory Provisions Requiring Public Notice and Comment of Applications.

The Marina Permit approved in the Secretary's Order is governed by the Marina Regulations, 7 Del. Admin. § 7501 *et seq*. Section 4.3.2.4 of those regulations provides:

> 4.3.2.4 Public Notice: Upon receipt of an application which is determined to be reasonably complete, the Department will:
>
> > 4.3.2.4.1 Advertise receipt of the application in two (2) newspapers of statewide circulation.
> >
> > 4.3.2.4.2 Receive public comments for 45 days from the date of notice.
> >
> > 4.3.2.4.3 Allow the applicant to respond to questions posed by the Department and the public within the time period defined for active applications.
> >
> > 4.3.2.4.4 Publish a public notice of the final completed application.
> >
> > 4.3.2.4.5 Receive requests for a public hearing and additional comments for 20 days from the date of notice.

The Subaqueous Land Lease approved in the Secretary's Order is governed by the provisions of the Subaqueous Lands Act, 7 Del. C. § 7201 *et seq*. Section 7207(a) of the Subaqueous Lands Act requires that persons seeking a lease of subaqueous lands must file an application with the Secretary, and § 7207(d) then provides:

> (d) Upon receipt of an application in proper form, the Secretary shall advertise in a daily newspaper of statewide circulation and in a newspaper of general circulation in the county in which the activity is proposed:
>
> > (1) The fact that the application has been received;
> >
> > (2) A brief description of the nature of the application; and
> >
> > (3) A statement that a public hearing may be requested by any interested person who offers a meritorious objection to the application.

The Secretary's Order makes clear that public notice and a public hearing was held on the original application filed by TAC Beacon 1, LLC. The Secretary's Order also makes clear that, *after* the public hearing and public comment was closed, and in response to public comment and input on the original application, TAC Beacon 1, LLC submitted a *revised* application that made significant changes to the proposed marina—as the Secretary's Order put it: "It should be noted that the design of this proposed project has been modified significantly by this Applicant from the application originally received by the Department." DNREC and the Secretary did not provide public notice, an opportunity for public comment, or the opportunity to request a public hearing on the revised application, despite the statutory and regulatory requires set forth above. In effect, the Secretary denied the public any opportunity to know about, see, comment on or receive a public hearing on the marina design that the Secretary and DNREC actually approved. As a result, the Secretary acted contrary to law.

B. The Secretary's Order, and the Approvals contained therein, Were Issued Without Compliance with Applicable Statutory and Regulatory Provisions Governing Leases of Subaqueous Lands.

In addition to the requirements of the Subaqueous Lands Act, requests for leases of subaqueous lands are subject to the Regulations Governing the Use of Subaqueous Lands, 7 Del. Admin. § 7504 *et seq*. In issuing the Secretary's Order and the Approvals contained therein, the Secretary acted arbitrarily, capriciously, and contrary to law in that the approvals do not comply with numerous sections of the Regulations Governing the Use of Subaqueous Lands. These sections include, but are not limited to, the following:

> *Section 4.2*: Section 4.2 states: "An application may be denied if the activity could cause harm to the environment, either singly or in combination with other activities or existing conditions, which cannot be mitigated sufficiently." DNREC and the Secretary failed to consider the harms to the environment from the construction of the marina, including the removal of trees and other measures that could contribute to erosion at the site;

Section 4.6: Section 4.6 states that DNREC "shall consider the public interest in any proposed activity which might affect the use of subaqueous lands," and lists numerous considerations thereunder. DNREC failed to or inadequately considered such impacts as effects on the environment/natural resources, navigation, recreation, aesthetic enjoyment, and the extent of public detriment from the project;

Section 4.7: Section 4.7 states that DNREC "shall consider the impact on the environment, and lists numerous considerations thereunder. DNREC failed to or inadequately considered such impacts as impairments to water quality, effects on recreational activities, and sediment transport functions, and the impacts when viewed in conjunction with other activities by the applicant, including the removal of trees and other measures that could contribute to erosion at the site;

C. The Secretary's Order, and the Approvals contained therein, Were Issued Without Compliance with Applicable Statutory and Regulatory Provisions Governing Marinas.

As noted above, the Marina Permit approved in the Secretary's Order is governed by the Marina Regulations, 7 Del. Admin. § 7501 *et seq*. In issuing the Secretary's Order and the Approvals contained therein, the Secretary acted arbitrarily, capriciously, and contrary to law in that the approvals do not comply with numerous sections of the Marina Regulations. These sections include, but are not limited to, the following:

Section 11.2.3: Section 11.2.3 requires DNREC to consider aspects of the public interest as part of the Review Criteria set forth in the Marina Regulations. DNREC failed to or inadequately considered the potential effects on the public interests with respect to navigation, recreation, aesthetic enjoyment, natural resources, and other uses of the subaqueous lands;

Section 11.3: Section 11.3 identifies environmental siting considerations that DNREC must consider in its permit review. DNREC failed to or inadequately considered the environmental siting considerations in this section including, but not limited to, water quality impacts, cumulative impacts, and wetlands; and

Section 11.4: Section 11.4 identifies planning and design requirements that DNREC must consider in its permit review. DNREC failed to or inadequately considered the planning and design requirements in this section including, but not limited to, navigation and access channels and vessel traffic and navigation, and sediment and erosion control.

IV. Estimate of Number of Witnesses and Time Involved [7]

Appellants estimate they may call all Appellants as witnesses for purposes of standing, and may call an additional 1 - 6 witnesses on the merits, which may include 1-2 experts. Appellants estimate that approximately 6 - 8 hours of hearing will be required for their case-in-chief exclusive of cross-examination. Appellants reserve the right to present additional witnesses as a result of the State's case.

Martin Lampner *et al.*

By: ______________________________

KENNETH T. KRISTL, ESQ. (DE Bar #5200)
Environmental & Natural Resources Law Clinic
Widener University Delaware Law School
4601 Concord Pike
Wilmington, DE 19803
(302) 477-2053
(302) 477-2032 (fax)
ktkristl@widener.edu

Counsel for Appellants

ANNOTATIONS FOR APPEXDIX TAB 4

[1] Addressed to the Environmental Appeals Board

[2] Identify the Secretary's action being appealed. Note that it spells out the Secretary Order's specific number (each Order has a unique number, all of which begin with the year in which the Order is issued, followed by letters that identify which Division is involved, and a unique #) as well as a narrative description of the project and what the Secretary's Order does (here, granting a Subaqueous Lands lease and a Marina Permit)

[3] Gives the name(s) of the party/ies appealing the Secretary's Order, as will as identification of the Secretary's Order and what it does.

[4] Satisfies the requirement to state the interest that is substantially affected [so as to claim standing]

[5] Alleges why the Secretary's Order was improperly issued. Note that the allegations here are summary in nature; the detailed explanation of each follows in the next section of the Statement of Appeal

[6] Detailed explanation of each allegation. Cites to applicable regulatory or statutory requirement and why the Secretary's Order fails to satisfy that requirement.

[7] Provides the number of witnesses and estimated time for trial as required by the Board's regulations.

APPENDIX TAB 5

Annotations on Sheet following the Notice of Appeal Document

Date Received (to be filled In by the Secretary) ________

Appeal Application Number (to be filled in by the Secretary) ________

RECEIVED
@5:26pm
JAN 13 2017
DNREC
SECRETARY'S OFFICE

STATE COASTAL ZONE INDUSTRIAL CONTROL BOARD
APPLICATION TO APPEAL FROM
A COASTAL ZONE ACT DECISION

[1]

Date January 12, 2017

Name of Appellant: **Delaware Audubon**
Address and Telephone Number: 56 W Main Street, Suite 212A, Christiana, DE 19702 302-292-3970

League of Women Voters of Delaware
Address and Telephone #: Clash Wing, Room 1, Lower Level, Wilmington, DE 19806 302-571-8948

A. Identify the Coastal Zone Decision Being Appealed

Secretary's Order 2016-CZ-0050 issued December 27, 2016 concerning Delaware City Refinery Company, LLC. And publicly noticed on January 1, 2017 (Copy attached)

[2]

B. Date of Public Notice of the Coastal Zone Decision________
(to be filled in by the Secretary)

C. Signature of Appellant or Appellant's Representative________
Kenneth T. Kristl, Esq.

Position or Title (if any) Counsel for Appellants

D. Briefly State the Reasons for Your Appeal. For example, if you believe the Decision is contrary to the Coastal Zone Act, identify those parts of the law involved and state why the Decision is contrary to them. Your Statement of Reasons for Appeal should be attached to this Application Form.

See attached [3]

Please include the appeal fee of One Hundred Dollars ($100) with this Appeal Application. The check or money order should be made out to: **Department of Natural Resources and Environmental Control**

Submit the completed Appeal Application, including the appeal fee, within fourteen (14) days following the public notice of the Coastal Zone Act decision to:

Chair
State Coastal Zone Industrial Control Board
c/o Department of Natural Resources and Environmental Control
89 Kings Highway
Dover, DE 19901

Reasons for Appeal to the Coastal Zone Industrial Control Board concerning Secretary's Order 2016-CZ-0050 concerning Delaware City Refinery Company, LLC.

Pursuant to *7 Del. C. §7007*, Delaware Audubon and League of Women Voters of Delaware (Appellants) submit these Reasons for Appeal as part of and attached to its Application to Appeal from a Coastal Zone Act Decision form. Appellants challenge the Secretary of the Delaware Department of Natural Resources and Environmental Control Order 2016-CZ-0050, issued December 27, 2016 and publicly noticed January 1, 2017 (Order), which grants Delaware City Refinery Company, LLC Coastal Zone Act Permit No. 427P (Permit) allowing the receipt and shipment of up to 10,000 barrels per day of ethanol from its facility located at 4550 Wrangle Hill Road, Delaware City, New Castle County (Refinery). Kenneth T. Kristl, Esq. of the Widener University Delaware Law School's Environmental and Natural Resources Law Clinic represents the Appellants in this matter.

Appellants ask the CZICB to reverse the Order and deny Coastal Zone Act Permit No. 427P (or, if deemed appropriate, to remand the Permit back to the Secretary) for one or more of the following reasons in the alternative:

1. In issuing the Order and Permit, the Secretary erred as a matter of law and fact in that the Order and Permit violate 7 Del. C. § 7003 and Section 4.2 of the CZA Regulations because that portion of the docking facility used to receive the ethanol is outside the footprint of the Refinery's nonconforming use as set forth in Appendix B to the CZA Regulations.

2. In issuing the Order and Permit, the Secretary erred as a matter of law and fact in that the Order and Permit violate 7 Del. C. § 7003 and Section 4.5 of the CZA Regulations because they allow a bulk product transfer facility that was not in operation on June 28, 1971.

3. In issuing the Order and Permit, the Secretary erred as a matter of law and fact in that the Order and Permit violate 7 Del. C. § 7003 and Section 4.6 of the CZA Regulations because they allow the conversion and use of an unregulated or exempted docking facility for the transfer of bulk products (i.e., ethanol).

4. In issuing the Order and Permit, the Secretary erred as a matter of law and fact in that the Secretary failed to consider all environmental impacts and effects on neighboring land uses—specifically, the environmental impacts and effects on neighboring land uses of shipping ethanol to the facility—as required by 7 Del. C. § 7004(a) and the Section 8.3.2 of the CZA Regulations.

5. In issuing the Order and Permit, the Secretary erred as a matter of law and fact in that the Secretary failed to consider any impacts of the proposed ethanol transfer activity on the Department's environmental goals for the Coastal Zone and the environmental indicators used to assess long-term environmental quality within the zone as required by the Section 8.3.3 of the CZA Regulations, given that the Department has never articulated nor adopted any such environmental indicators.

6. In issuing the Order and Permit, the Secretary erred as a matter of law and fact in that the Secretary failed to use a set of prioritized environmental indicators as a tool for assessing environmental impacts as required by Sections 5.3 and 5.4 of the DNREC guidance found at

"Appendix C to the Regulations Governing Delaware's Coastal Zone," given that the Department has never articulated nor adopted any such environmental indicators.

7. In issuing the Order and Permit, the Secretary erred as a matter of law and fact in that the Secretary failed to include well-defined and measurable commitments or accomplishments concerning the proposed offset proposal that are independently auditable by the Department and available to the public via the Freedom of Information Act and failed to include inspection, reporting and notification obligations in the permit concerning the offset proposal as required by Section 5.8 of the DNREC guidance found at "Appendix C to the Regulations Governing Delaware's Coastal Zone."

ANNOTATIONS FOR APPEXDIX TAB 5

[1] Notice of Appeal Form of the Coastal Zone Industrial Control Board used in past. Technically, the Board only requires the filing of a Notice of Appeal, so you could file without using the form. A blank copy of the form follows this Annotation.

[2] Note that a copy of the Secretary's decision is attached to the Notice.

[3] If using the Form, you can attach the statement of reasons to the form.

[4] Identify all of the reasons that appellant contents the Secretary's Order was improper. Note the citation to specific regulatory sections within the reasons presented.

Date Received (to be filled
In by the Secretary)

Appeal Application Number (to
be filled in by the Secretary)

STATE COASTAL ZONE INDUSTRIAL CONTROL BOARD
APPLICATION TO APPEAL FROM
A COASTAL ZONE ACT DECISION

Date

Name of Appellant:
Address and Telephone Number:

A. **Identify the Coastal Zone Decision Being Appealed**

B. **Date of Public Notice of the Coastal Zone Decision**______________________________
(to be filled in by the Secretary)

C. **Signature of Appellant or Appellant's Representative**______________________________

Position or Title (if any)____

D. **Briefly State the Reasons for Your Appeal. For example, if you believe the Decision is contrary to the Coastal Zone Act, identify those parts of the law involved and state why the Decision is contrary to them. Your Statement of Reasons for Appeal should be attached to this Application Form.**

Please include the appeal fee of One Hundred Dollars ($100) with this Appeal Application. The check or money order should be made out to: **Department of Natural Resources and Environmental Control**

Submit the completed Appeal Application, including the appeal fee, within fourteen (14) days following the public notice of the Coastal Zone Act decision to:

Chair
State Coastal Zone Industrial Control Board
c/o Department of Natural Resources and Environmental Control
89 Kings Highway

Dover, DE 19901

APPENDIX TAB 6

Stipulation of Facts Example Documents

BEFORE THE ENVIRONMENTAL APPEALS BOARD
OF THE STATE OF DELAWARE

MARTIN LAMPNER, et. al.,

Appellants,

v.

DELAWARE DEPARTMENT OF NATURAL RESOURCES AND ENVIRONMENTAL CONTROL,

Appellee.

[1]

EAB Docket No. 2019-02

STIPULATION OF THE PARTIES FOR THE JULY 9, 2019 HEARING [2]

Appellants Martin Lampner, *et.al.* ("Appellants") and Appellee Delaware Department of Natural Resources and Environmental Control ("DNREC"), by and through their respective counsels, hereby stipulate and agree to the following for purposes of the July 9, 2019 Hearing before the Board in this appeal:

[3] 1. Appellants have standing to bring this appeal because each Appellant has an interest that is substantially affected by the Secretary's decision at issue in this appeal.

2. On or about November 16, 2016, TAC Beacon 1, LLC ("TAC Beacon") submitted an application for a Marina Permit and Subaqueous Lands Lease (Chronology Exhibit 1) ("November 2016 Application") to DNREC.

3. DNREC issued notice of a public hearing on the November 2016 Application (Chronology Exhibit 4) and held the public hearing on June 6, 2017 (Chronology Exhibit 6 is the Transcript of the June 6, 2017 public hearing).

4. On or about July 31, 2017, after the June 6, 2017 public hearing had been held and the public comment period had closed, TAC Beacon submitted a revised application to DNREC ("July 2017 Application") (Chronology Exhibit 7).

5. DNREC did not issue public notice of its receipt of the July 2017 Application.

6. DNREC did not notify the public that public comment on the July 2017 Application could be submitted to DNREC.

7. DNREC did not notify the public that a public hearing could be requested on the July 2017 Application.

8. DNREC did not hold a public hearing on the July 2017 Application.

9. Appellants Anthony Debartolomeo, Wanda Debartolomeo, Peter Cramer, and Timothy Saxton hereby withdraw their individual appeals in this matter.

SO AGREED AND STIPULATED.

DATED: June 27, 2019

[4]

/s/ Kenneth T. Kristl
Kenneth T. Kristl, Esq.
Widener Environmental & Natural
Resources Law Clinic
4601 Concord Pike
Wilmington, DE 19803
(302) 477-2053
ktkristl@widener.edu

/s/ Kayli Spialter*
Kayli Spialter, Esq.
Deputy Attorney General
Department of Justice
820 North French Street
Wilmington, DE 19801
(302) 577-8508
Kayli.spialter@delaware.gov

* *Permission to e-sign granted via Email on June 27, 2019*

BEFORE THE COASTAL ZONE INDUSTRIAL CONTROL BOARD FOR THE STATE OF DELAWARE

DELAWARE AUDUBON and LEAGUE OF WOMEN VOTERS OF DELAWARE, Appellants, v. DELAWARE DEPARTMENT OF NATURAL RESOURCES AND ENVIRONMENTAL CONTROL, Appellee, and DELAWARE CITY REFINING COMPANY LLC, Intervenor/Appellee.	)	Appeal No. 2017-01

JOINT FINAL PRE-HEARING ORDER

In accordance with the January 30, 2017 Scheduling Order ("Scheduling Order") issued by the Coastal Zone Industrial Control Board (the "Board"), the Appellants Delaware Audubon and League of Women Voters of Delaware (the "Appellants"), Appellee Delaware Department of Natural Resources and Environmental Control ("DNREC" or the "Department"), and Intervenor/Appellee Delaware City Refining Company LLC ("DCRC") (collectively, the "Parties") hereby jointly submit the following Final Pre-Hearing Order for the above-captioned matter (the "Pre-Hearing Order"). The Pre-Hearing Order shall govern the conduct of the hearing of this case. Amendments to this order will be allowed only in exceptional circumstances to prevent manifest injustice.

1. Nature of the Action DCRC's Motion to Intervene the Parties' Pre-Hearin Memoranda, and DNREC's and DCRC's Motions to Dismiss

This appeal to the Board was filed by Appellants on January 17, 2017 (the "Appeal"). The Appeal challenges Coastal Zone Permit No. 427 and associated Secretary's Order No. 2016-CZ-0050 (the "Secretary's Order) (together, with Coastal Zone Permit No. 427, the "CZA Permit" or the "Permit"), dated December 27, 2016. The CZA Permit authorizes DCRC to use existing tanks and existing marine loading equipment at its existing refinery located at 4550

Wrangle Hill Road, Delaware City 19706 (the "Refinery"), to enable up to 10,000 barrels per day ("BPD") (on an annual average basis) of denatured ethanol (herein, "ethanol") to be loaded from storage tanks to marine vessels and shipped to offsite facilities. The Appeal alleges that the CZA Permit violates the Coastal Zone Act, 7 Del. C. § 7001 *et seq.* (the "CZA") and the Coastal Zone Act Regulations, 7 Del. Admin. 101 ("CZA Regulations"). On January 18, DCRC filed a motion to intervene in the above-captioned case with the Board. On January 20, 2017, the Board Chair granted DCRC's motion to intervene.

Appellants filed with the Board their Pre-Hearing Memo in support of the Appeal on January 30, 2017. On February 7, 2017, DNREC and DCRC filed their individual Pre-Hearing Memoranda, presenting, respectively, DNREC's and DCRC's legal and factual arguments in response to the Appeal and Appellants' Pre-Hearing Memo.

On February 10, 2017, DNREC and DCRC each filed a Motion to Dismiss and opening brief, requesting that the Board dismiss Appeal Grounds 1, 4, 5, 6, and 7 of the Appeal. On February 15, 2017, Appellants filed an answering brief in opposition to DNREC's and DCRC's Motions to Dismiss. The respective positions of DNREC, DCRC, and Appellants on the issues addressed in DNREC's and DCRC's Motions to Dismiss, and Appellants' answer thereto, are set forth in the Parties' opening and answering briefs relating to the motions.

2. **Factual Contentions of Appellants Delaware Audubon and League of Women Voters of Delaware**

The following include some, but not necessarily all, of the facts that Appellants intend to prove at the hearing:

A. The Memorandum of Understanding from which the CZA Regulations arose provided for and depended on the creation and use of environmental goals and indicators by DNREC.

B. The approval of the CZA Regulations depended on the creation and use of environmental goals and indicators by DNREC.

C. The Permit does not contain any requirements to monitor, measure, or report air emissions from activity under the Permit or the Offset Proposal approved under the Permit.

D. The Refinery did not ship ethanol from its docks and piers prior to 2006.

E. In issuing the Permit, the Secretary did not consider the impacts of air emissions from the trains that bring ethanol to the Refinery for shipment under the Permit and/or the air emissions from marine vessels which will transport ethanol from the Refinery under the Permit.

F. In issuing the Permit, the Secretary did not consider the impacts of noise from the trains that bring ethanol to the Refinery for shipment under the Permit and/or the noise from marine vessels which will transport ethanol from the Refinery under the Permit.

G. In issuing the Permit, the Secretary did not consider the impacts of the proposed activity on the environmental goals under the Coastal Zone Act.

H. In issuing the Permit, the Secretary did not consider the impacts of the proposed activity on the environmental indicators as described in the Memorandum of Understanding and Appendix C to the CZA Regulations.

3. Factual Contentions of Intervenor/Appellee Delaware City Refining Company

The following include some, but not necessarily all, of the facts that DCRC intends to prove at the hearing:

A. Throughout the operating history of the Refinery, processed and unprocessed petroleum-related materials, including raw materials, intermediates, and finished products, have been received at and shipped from the Refinery through multiple logistic and support systems, including via marine vessel, rail, truck, and pipeline.

B. The Refinery has throughout its history shipped raw materials, intermediates such as gasoline additives, and finished products from the Refinery to various destinations for many reasons.

C. It is integral to the functionality of the Refinery to move petroleum-related materials, including raw materials, intermediates, and finished products to, within, and from the Refinery, as dictated by economic, operational, and logistical factors.

D. The Refinery has throughout its history shipped raw materials, intermediates such as gasoline additives, and finished products from the Refinery to various destinations for many reasons. Depending on market and operational factors, materials have been received at and shipped from the Refinery without prior processing or use at the Facility. The Refinery has also purchased refining-related materials for the intended purpose of reselling the materials without prior processing.

E. As described in Paragraph 5.P., the Delaware Office of Management, Budget, and Planning issued to the Refinery a Status Decision authorizing the construction and operation of a methanol production plant at the Refinery without a CZA permit. The purpose of the methanol plant, as identified in the Refinery's application for status decision, was to produce methanol both for on-site use in gasoline blending activities, and for sale and off-site shipment by marine vessel to other facilities.

F. The East rail rack (the "East Rack") has been in operation at the Refinery since approximately 1956 for the purpose of receiving materials via rail from multiple sources. Following offloading of materials from rail cars at the East Rack, materials are transferred into tankage at the Refinery, and later directed to other equipment at the Refinery for processing, blending, temporary storage, or transfer to other locations or other vessels, including barges.

G. The rail cars and locomotives delivering ethanol to the East Rack are operated by Norfolk-Southern Railway, as confirmed through various contractual agreements executed by DCRC and Norfolk Southern Company.

H. DCRC addresses through the CZA Permit Application the application to the Project of the six factors enumerated in Section 7004(b) of the CZA. (See description of defined terms the "CZA Permit Application" and the "Project" in Paragraph 5.V.)

I. The CZA Permit Application also describes that ethanol received at the East Rack would be transferred by existing piping to either of two existing Refinery storage tanks, identified as TK-206 and TK-225. Only minor adjustments to existing piping networks would be needed to transfer ethanol to the tanks.

J. The CZA Permit Application also describes that the Project would include the transfer of ethanol from TK-206 or TK-225 either to the existing Refinery blending operation or to the Docking Facility, in either case using existing piping. The piping dedicated to the Docking Facility had been previously installed for the movement of methanol from the on-site production plant to the Docking Facility (see Paragraph 5.P.).

K. The CZA Permit Application also describes that ethanol will be loaded onto marine vessels at the Docking Facility using existing material loading equipment at the existing berths. (See description of defined term the "Docking Facility" in Paragraph 5.M.)

L. The CZA Permit Application also describes that the volatile organic compound ("VOC") emissions displaced during ethanol loading to the marine vessels will be controlled by the existing MVRS. The CZA Permit Application reports that the projected emissions following control by the MVRS would require no increase in existing emission levels identified in the air quality permit for this air pollution control device. (See description of defined term the "MVRS" in Paragraph 5.O.)

M. The CZA Permit Application also describes that the aggregate projected air emissions for the Project -- associated with management of ethanol within the Refinery (notably including within and through the storage tanks) and the ethanol loading activities -- are less than 1 ton per year.

N. The CZA Permit Application further describes that the aggregate allowable VOC emission increases related to the Project will be more than offset by the installation and operation of a new vapor capture system ("VCS") at a separate truck loading terminal ("Truck Loading Terminal").

O. The CZA Permit Application addresses the environmental impacts of the Project as follows:

1. Project will not increase the allowable quantity of marine vessel loading at the Docking Facility.

2. The Project will not require the construction of any new water intakes on the Delaware River, nor any increase in flow at the existing water intake on the river.

P. The Project will not result in an increase in wastewater discharges from the Refinery to the Delaware River.

Q. The proposed activity covered by the Project is incidental to the Facility's historic operations governing the management of petroleum-related materials and off-site transfer of materials without prior processing.

R. On or about August 18, 2016, the Refinery submitted an air permit application package to DNREC's Division of Air Quality relating to the Project (the "Air Permit Application"). A copy of the Air Permit Application is Exhibit IA12.

S. The CZA Permit reflects DNREC's conclusions that the Project will result in a net environmental benefit.

T. The Air Permit Application requested authorization for a small increase in the previously established tank-specific emission limits for TK-206 to accommodate the increased ethanol throughput, and for a minor air emission limit authorization to repurpose existing tank TK-225 for ethanol service; minor instrumentation changes to the MVRS; and, minor modifications at the Truck Loading Rack to allow for the installation and operation of the VCS and loading to the trucks. The Air Permit Application requested no increase in allowable throughput for loading of marine vessels at the Docking Facility.

U. DNREC determined that the Air Permit Application Package was administratively complete and published notice of DNREC's intent to issue the related air permits.

V. In response to the Air Permit Application Package, DNREC issued two draft air permits: one permit governing the minor modifications associated with the use of existing Refinery tanks and marine loading equipment to enable ethanol to be loaded from storage tanks to marine vessels (the "Draft Project Air Permit"); and a second permit governing the installation and operation of the VCS offset project at the Truck Loading Terminal (the "Draft Offset Air Permit"). Copies of the Draft Project Air Permit and the Draft Offset Air Permit are Exhibits IA13 and IA14, respectively.

W. On January 15, 2017, DNREC published notice of the Draft Project Air Permit (identified as Permit APC-1995/0471-CONSTRUCTION/OPERATION (A5)(LAER)(MACT)(NSPS) – MVRS; APC-1980/0868-CONSTRUCTION/OPERATION (A5)(MACT)(VOC RACT) – Tank 206; APC-1980/0869-CONSTRUCTION/OPERATION (A7)(MACT)(VOC RACT) – Tank 225) and Draft Offset Air Permit (identified as Permit APC-1988/0125-CONSTRUCTION (Amendment 6)(MACT)).

X. The Draft Offset Air Permit establishes applicable emission standards and operating limitations and related compliance demonstration requirements for the offset project.

4. **Factual Contentions of Appellee DNREC**

The following include some, but not necessarily all, of the facts that DNREC intends to prove at the hearing:

A. In addition to the facts relating to the operation of the Refinery and its Docking Facility to be presented by DCRC, DNREC will prove that the maximum throughput of 10,000 BPD of ethanol to be shipped from the Docking Facility as a result of the Permit represents a small portion of the Refinery's crude unit throughput benchmark of 191,100 BPD.

B. Prior to issuing the Permit, DNREC appropriately considered all the factors set forth in Section 7004(b) of the CZA, as well as the issues addressed in the permit application and the concerns raised at the public hearing on the Permit application.

C. The Permit requires the installation and maintenance of a new vapor capture system at the Refinery's truck loading terminal that will reduce air emissions of volatile organic compounds ("VOCs") by anywhere between 17 and 26.9 tons per year.

D. The allocation of 1.1 tons per year of reduction in VOCs resulting from the installation of a new vapor capture system, as required by the Order and Permit, will more than offset the negative environmental impacts likely to be generated by the new activity, including, as the primary impact, an increase of 0.8 tons per year of VOCs associated with increased loading of ethanol into storage tanks at the Refinery.

E. DNREC considered the CZA permit application in light of environmental goals relating to improving air quality, water quality, habitat/land cover, and living resources.

F. In the event that Grounds 5 and 6 of the appeal, relating to environmental indicators, survive the motions to dismiss and motions in limine, DNREC will show that previous administrations concluded that the formal adoption and maintenance of indicators was unworkable and inadvisable, and that regulation under the CZA has nevertheless been successful, including with respect to ensuring that environmental impacts are more than offset by an applicant's offset proposal.

G. In the event that Appellants' Ground 7 of the appeal, relating to Section 5.8 of the DNREC Guidance, survives DNREC's motion to dismiss and motion in limine, DNREC will show that the Permit is consistent with the non-binding guidance set forth in Section 5.8.

5. **Stipulated Facts**

Without conceding the legal significance, effect, relevance, and/or materiality thereof, and reserving the right to argue the legal significance, effect, relevance and/or materiality thereof, the parties stipulate to the following facts for purposes of this appeal:

A. Intervenor/Appellee DCRC is the current owner and operator of the Refinery, with an address of 4550 Wrangle Hill Road, Delaware City 19706.

B. The Refinery commenced operation as a petroleum refinery in 1956.

C. The Refinery has operated as a petroleum refinery since its initial operation.

D. The Refinery did not ship denatured ethanol in bulk quantities from its piers and docks on or prior to June 28, 1971.

E. All ethanol that is transported to the Refinery by rail and subsequently shipped from the Refinery as authorized by the Permit will be unloaded at the Refinery's East Rack rail facility.

F. Although trains bringing ethanol to the Refinery to be shipped from the Refinery as authorized by the Permit generate air emissions, the Project authorized by the Permit does not involve any increase in the number of train cars that the Refinery can receive for unloading of cargo, which is otherwise limited both by regulatory-based restrictions on air emissions relevant to the rail unloading activities and by the available logistical capacity at the Refinery to receive trains for unloading of cargo.

G. Although marine vessels that will transport ethanol from the Refinery as authorized by the Permit generate air emissions, the Project authorized by the Permit does not involve any increase in the Refinery's capacity to load/unload or otherwise accommodate marine vessels at the Docking Facility, which is otherwise limited both by applicable permit-based restrictions on air emissions relevant to marine vessel loading/unloading activities and by the Refinery's available logistical capacity to load/unload marine vessels at the Docking Facility.

H. Although trains bringing ethanol to the Refinery to be shipped from the Refinery as authorized by the Permit generate noise, the Project authorized by the Permit does not involve any increase in the number of train cars that the Refinery can receive for unloading of cargo, which is otherwise limited both by regulatory-based restrictions on air emission relevant to the rail unloading activities and by the available logistical capacity at the Refinery to receive trains for unloading of cargo.

I. Although marine vessels that will transport ethanol from the Refinery as authorized by the Permit generate noise, the Project authorized by the Permit does not involve any increase in the Refinery's capacity to load/unload or otherwise accommodate marine vessels at the Docking Facility, which is otherwise limited both by applicable permit-based restrictions on air emissions relevant to marine vessel loading/unloading activities and by the Refinery's available logistical capacity to load/unload marine vessels at the Docking Facility.

J. DNREC has adopted environmental goals but has not adopted a final set of environmental indicators as described in Appendix C to the CZA Regulations for use in reviewing permit applications under the Coastal Zone Act.

K. Appellants filed their appeal after the close of business hours on Friday, January 14, 2017, and so, given the intervening weekend and holiday, the filing is considered to have occurred on January 17, 2017. Public notice of the CZA Permit was published on January 1, 2017. DNREC and DCRC agree to the treatment of the Appeal filing date as January 17, and do not assert any objection to the timeliness of the Appeal on that basis (but do not thereby waive any argument otherwise available based on the timing of the actual receipt of the Appeal).

L. The CZA was adopted on or about June 28, 1971.

M. The Refinery includes a docking facility consisting of three docks and associated supporting and other structures and equipment located at or adjacent to the docks and used to transfer petroleum materials across the docks to and from marine vessels, including barges (the "Docking Facility").

N. The Docking Facility has been in operation at the Refinery since approximately 1956.

O. The Docking Facility uses air pollution control equipment, known as the Marine Vapor Recovery System ("MVRS"), to capture vapors displaced during certain transfers of petroleum materials across the docks between marine vessels and the Refinery.

P. On November 14, 1980, the Delaware Office of Management, Budget, and Planning (which was charged with making CZA decisions prior to DNREC's creation) issued to the Refinery a Status Decision deciding that the Refinery was authorized under the CZA to construct and operate a methanol production plant at the Refinery without the need to secure a permit under the CZA (the "Methanol Plant Status Decision"). A copy of the Methanol Plant Status Decision is Exhibit IA8.

Q. On July 20, 1998, DNREC issued to the Refinery a Status Decision (the "RFG Status Decision") deciding that a CZA permit was not required for the installation and utilization of new process equipment at the Refinery to reformulate gasoline to comply with the new federal standards for reformulated gasoline ("RFG"). A copy of the RFG Status Decision is Exhibit IA9.

R. On March 3, 2006, DNREC issued to the Refinery a Status Decision confirming that the Refinery was authorized under the CZA to receive ethanol via marine vessel at the Refinery's Docking Facility without the need to secure a permit under the CZA (the "2006 Ethanol Status Decision"). The Refinery's request for status decision explained that the ethanol would be used as a gasoline additive in the Refinery's gasoline blending operations. A copy of the 2006 Ethanol Status Decision is Exhibit IA10.

S. In accordance with the 2006 Ethanol Status Decision, the Refinery has received ethanol by barge since 2006.

T. Consistent with current federal air quality standards, the Refinery manages ethanol as the current type of fuel additive blended with gasoline to achieve reduced emission levels.

U. Appendix B of the CZA Regulations identifies the Refinery's pre-1971, nonconforming footprint (the "Refinery's CZA Footprint").

V. On August 18, 2016, the Refinery submitted to DNREC an application for a CZA permit (the "CZA Permit Application") to address the activities at the Refinery supporting the proposed transfer of ethanol from existing storage tanks to marine vessels, using the existing marine loading equipment at the Docking Facility, related to the shipment of ethanol to off-site locations (the "Project"). A copy of the CZA Permit Application is Chronology Tab A.

W. Legal notices announcing the receipt and availability of the CZA Permit Application were published in the News Journal and New Castle Weekly on August 28 and August 31, 2016, respectively.

X. The Secretary of DNREC signed the Secretary's Environmental Assessment Report on September 28, 2016, deeming the application preliminarily administratively complete and ready to proceed to a public hearing.

Y. Legal notices announcing the public hearing and the availability of the CZA Permit Application were published in the News Journal and New Castle Weekly on October 2 and October 5, 2016, respectively.

Z. On or about October 28, 2016, DNREC held a public hearing on the CZA Permit Application. A transcript of that hearing is Chronology Tab C.

AA. The Project will not result in the construction of any new pier nor extension of the existing piers at the Docking Facility.

BB. The Project will not expand the Refinery or the Docking Facility beyond the Refinery's CZA Footprint.

CC. The processing of crude oil at the Refinery initiates at a process unit known as the "Crude Unit." On January 24, 2005, DNREC issued an amendment to Coastal Zone Act Permit No. 355 for the Refinery, identifying a throughput rate for the Crude Unit of 191,100 BPD as the benchmark for evaluating any future increases in processing rate at the Refinery. The Project will not expand or increase the total throughput of crude that is processed at the Refinery.

DD. On or about December 27, 2016, DNREC issued to the Refinery the CZA Permit, expressly authorizing "[t]he utilization of existing tanks and existing marine loading equipment at [the Refinery] to enable denatured ethanol to be loaded from storage tanks to marine vessels and shipped to offsite facilities." A copy of the CZA Permit is Chronology Tab N.

EE. On or about December 27, 2016, the Hearing Officer issued his Hearing Officer's Report on the CZA Permit Application. The Hearing Officer's Report is Chronology Tab M.

FF. On or about December 27, 2016, DNREC issued its Technical Response Memorandum ("TRM") for the CZA Permit. The TRM includes DNREC's consideration of the six statutory criteria under Section 7004(b) of the CZA. The TRM is Chronology Tab L.

GG. The CZA Permit expressly requires that the VCS offset project be implemented at the Truck Loading Rack before the ethanol loading activities authorized through the CZA Permit may begin.

6. **Statement of Legal Issues Presented**

The parties jointly agree that the Appeal presents the following legal issues:

1. Whether, as the Secretary concluded in his Order, the Project represents an allowable expansion of a legally existing nonconforming heavy industry use under Section 7004(a) of the CZA and Section 6.3 of the CZA Regulations that is subject to the permitting requirements in CZA Section 7004(b) or whether, as Appellants contend, the Project represents the establishment of a new bulk product transfer facility, or the conversion or use of the Docking Facility to a new bulk product transfer facility, contrary to the provisions of Section 7003 of the CZA and Sections 4.5 and/or 4.6 of the CZA Regulations. (See Appeal Grounds 2 and 3).

2. Whether the Secretary's decision to issue the Permit properly reflected consideration of the environmental impacts and any effects on neighboring land uses of the Project. (See Appeal Ground 4).

3. Whether the Secretary's issuance of the Permit is inconsistent with Section 8.3.3 of the CZA Regulations, relating to environmental goals and indicators, and if so, whether such inconsistency warrants denial of the Permit. (See Appeal Ground 5).

4. Whether the Secretary's issuance of the Permit violated the CZA, based on Sections 5.3 and 5.4 of the DNREC guidance attached as Appendix C to the Regulations governing Delaware's Coastal Zone ("Guidance"), relating to environmental goals and indicators, and if so, whether such violation warrants denial of the Permit. (See Appeal Ground 6).

5. Whether the Secretary's issuance of the CZA Permit violated the CZA, based on Section 5.8 of the Guidance, relating to environmental offsets, and if so, whether such violation warrants denial of the Permit. (See Appeal Ground 7).

7. **Exhibits**

(Each party shall list separately and describe with particularity each exhibit which it intends to use at the hearing. Except for exhibits used on rebuttal, any exhibit not listed may not be used during the parties' case-in-chief, unless the existence of the exhibit, despite due diligence, was unknown to the party and its counsel at the time of submission of this order. If a party intends to use no exhibits at the hearing for any purpose, the party shall so state. Exhibits should be pre-marked prior to the hearing.)

All parties reserve the right to raise any objections as to any listed Exhibit, and/or to argue the legal effect and significance of any listed Exhibit.

A. Appellants Delaware Audubon and League of Women Voters of Delaware:

Appellants' Exhibits are identified as follows:

Appellants' Exhibit #	Description
1	Affidavit of Matthew DelPizzo
2	Affidavit of Jill Fuchs
3	March 18, 1998 Memorandum of Understanding of the Delaware Coastal Zone Regulatory Advisory Committee to the Delaware Department of Natural Resources and Environmental Control (MOU)
4	Affidavit of Debbie Heaton
5	Order of the Coastal Zone Industrial Control Board adopting the CZA Regulations from 2 Del. Reg. 2133 (May 1, 1999)
6	CZA Regulations (taken from DNREC's website)
7	Application of Premcor Refining Group for Coastal Zone Status Decision received December 22, 2005 and March 3, 2006 Status Decision concerning use of ethanol at the Refinery
8	PBF Energy, Inc. Presentation at Barclays CEO Energy-Power Conference, September 2016
9	December 23, 2016 Notice of Violation to DCRC from DNREC
10	Set of printouts from DNREC website re environment releases/violations from the Refinery
11	Cover and excerpts from PBF Logistics LP Form 10-Q filed with the Securities and Exchange Commission November 4, 2016 for the period ended September 30, 2016 (TOC and pp. 38-43)
13	May 18, 2012 Letter from Mark Chernaik, Ph.D. to Sara Bucic, Delaware City Environmental Coalition re results of pre- and post-startup air sampling
14	November 2, 2012 Letter from David Carter, Conservation Chair, Delaware Audubon to Colin O'Mara, Secretary of DNREC re Delaware City Air Quality Monitoring and Delaware Coastal Zone

	Environmental Indicators Implementation
15	March 10-11, 2016 DNREC Emails
16	March 24, 2016 DNREC Emails
17	June 9, 2016 DNREC Emails

The Parties do not object to the admissibility of Appellants' Exhibit Nos. 3, 5-9, 11, and 14-17, with respect to the foundation and/or authenticity of such Exhibits.

In addition, Appellants may use documents identified in the Chronology prepared for this matter. Appellants reserve the right to use any document identified by DNREC or DCRC as an exhibit in their case-in-chief.

B. Intervenor DCRC:

DCRC's Exhibits are identified as follows:

Intervenor/Appellee's Exhibit #	Description
IA1	CV of Scott Gerbman
IA2	CV of Michael Smith
IA3	Refinery Process Schematic #1
IA4	Refinery Process Schematic #2
IA5	History of Gasoline Additives
IA6	Refinery Site Plan
IA7	Process flow diagram for Project from CZA Permit Application
IA8	November 14, 1980 Coastal Zone Act Status Decision issued to Refinery regarding proposed methanol plant project
IA9	July 20, 1998 Coastal Zone Act Status Decision issued to Refinery regarding proposed reformulated gasoline project
IA10	March 3, 2006 Coastal Zone Act Status Decision issued to Refinery regarding proposed ethanol project
IA11	Title V Air Operating Permit provisions governing MVRS
IA12	August 18, 2016 air permit application addressing Project, submitted by Refinery to DNREC's Division of Air Quality
IA13	February 2017 Draft Project Air Permit
IA14	February 2017 Draft Offset Air Permit
IA15	Equipment Photo #1
IA16	Equipment Photo #2
IA17	Equipment Photo #3
IA18	Equipment Photo #4
IA19	Equipment Photo #5
IA20	Equipment Photo #6

In addition, DCRC may use documents identified in the Chronology prepared for this matter. DCRC reserves the right to use any document identified by Appellants or DNREC as an exhibit in its case-in-chief.

C. Appellee DNREC:

DNREC's Exhibits are identified as follows:

DNREC Exhibit #	Description
DNREC 1	The Coastal Zone Act
DNREC 2	Coastal Zone Regulations, including Appendix B thereto
DNREC 3	Newspaper Articles and Excerpt from Tidewater Oil Company 1956 Annual Report (Delaware Public Archives), 1956
DNREC 4	Oil and Gas Journal – Dedication Issue – Tidewater Oil Company, May 27, 1957
DNREC 5	Original Marine Vapor Recovery System Air Permit, July 1, 1998
DNREC 6	DNREC First Coastal Zone Act Assessment Report, May 11, 2000
DNREC 7	Letter from Amy Roe to Governor Markell, July 16, 2012
DNREC 8	Letter from Former Secretary O'Mara's to Amy Roe, August 6, 2012
DNREC 9	Email from Secretary O'Mara to David Carter, October 2, 2012
DNREC 10	Permit Amendment for Marine Vapor Recovery System at DCRC Piers 2 and 3, May 31, 2013
DNREC 11	Transcript of Hearing before the CZICB, July 16, 2013
DNREC 12	Updated Air Registration for Ethanol Offloading from Railcars at East Rack, March 7, 2016
DNREC 13	Picture of DCRC Refinery (Google Earth, May 24, 2016)
DNREC 14	Picture of DCRC Docking Facility (Google Earth, May 24, 2016)
DNREC 15	DCRC Ethanol Marketing Project Air Permit Application, August 2016
DNREC 16	Air Permit Response Memorandum from Lindsay Rennie to Angela D. Marconi, P.E., BCEE, January 17, 2017
DNREC 17	Appendix to DNREC's Pre-hearing Memorandum (previously submitted Feb. 7, 2017)
DNREC 18	Draft Air Permit – Delaware City Sales Terminal, February 2017
DNREC 19	Draft Air Permit – Delaware City Refinery – Ethanol Marketing Project, February 2017

In addition, DNREC may use documents identified in the Chronology prepared for this matter. DNREC reserves the right to use any document identified by Appellants or DCRC as an exhibit in its case-in-chief.

8. **Expert Witnesses**

A. Appellants Delaware Audubon and League of Women Voters:

Appellants do not anticipate calling any expert witnesses in its case-in-chief.

B. Intervenor/Appellee DCRC:

1. **Michael Smith** will serve as an expert witness addressing historic and current practices regarding the management of petroleum-related constituents, including without limitation, feedstocks, blending agents, intermediates, and partially refined and finished products associated with petroleum refining and process operations.

2. **Scott Gerbman** will serve as an expert witness addressing the use at petroleum refineries of different gasoline additives over time.

C. Appellee DNREC:

DNREC will not present any testimony from expert witnesses

. **Fact Witnesses**

(The name of each witness whom the party intends to call at the hearing shall be listed ith a short identifying statement. A summary of the anticipated testimony of each witness must be provided. Except for rebuttal witnesses, no party shall call a witness at the hearing whose name does not appear on that party's witness list, unless the existence of the potential witness was unknown to the party, despite due diligence, at the time of submission of this order. Upon the discovery of a new witness, the name of such witness and a summary of the testimony shall be seasonably supplied to all parties.)

A. Appellants Delaware Audubon and League of Women Voters of Delaware:

Appellants may call one or more of the following witnesses in its case-in-chief:

1. **David Carter** – standing, environmental impacts, DNREC failure to develop environmental indicators, (if needed, Appendix B issues re Double Loop Track)

2. **Mark Martell** – standing, environmental impacts, Audubon development of Pea Patch Island heronry

3. **Peggy Schultz** – standing, environmental impacts

4. **Bernard August** –standing, environmental impacts

5. **Suzanne Poitras**—standing, environmental impacts

6. **Victor Singer**—Board's approval of CZA Regulations and role of environmental indicators

7. **Matthew DelPizzo**—standing, environmental impacts, Audubon development and use of Pea Patch Island heronry

8. **Linda DelPizzo**—standing, environmental impacts

B. Intervenor/Appellee DCRC:

DCRC may call one or more of the following witnesses in its case-in-chief:

1. **Tom Godlewski** is the Environmental Manager for the Refinery and will address the elements of the ethanol project, the environmental review of project activities, and the permitting activity associated with the instant Coastal Zone Permit appeal.

2. **Michael Gudgeon** is the Technical Manager for the Refinery and will address technical- and process-specific considerations related to the movement of materials to, from, and within the Refinery, including raw materials, intermediates, and finished products, as well as the management of materials at the Refinery.

3. **Pat Kennedy** has held several positions at the Refinery commencing in the 1970's, and is currently a Director of Logistics. Pat will address relevant historic refinery activities, logistical considerations related to the movement of materials to, from, and within the Refinery, including raw materials, intermediates, and finished products, and equipment and operational considerations associated with the ethanol project.

4. **Mari-Kate Alter** is the Manager of Economics and Planning for the Refinery and will speak to economic and planning considerations relevant to the purchase, sale and movement of materials to, from, and within the Refinery, including raw materials, intermediates, and finished products.

C. Appellee DNREC:

Depending upon the evidence presented by the other parties, DNREC may or may not call the following witnesses to testify as to the matters indicated below:

1. **Susan E. Love**, Climate & Sustainability Section Lead, DNREC Division of Energy & Climate (Coastal Zone Act Program) (environmental goals and indicators; the CZA permit process; the Technical Response Memorandum, and related issues).

2. **Kevin F. Coyle**, Principal Planner, DNREC Division of Energy and Climate (Coastal Zone Act Program) (environmental goals and indicators; the CZA permit process; the Technical Response Memorandum, and related issues).

3. **Jamie Bethard**, Chief, Environmental Program Manager II, DNREC Emergency Prevention and Response (emergency response procedures; properties of ethanol)

4. **Ravi Rangan, P.E.**, Engineer VI, DNREC Division of Air Quality (operations at the Refinery; DNREC monitoring of operations at the Refinery; DAQ involvement in CZA permit request process and related air permit request; and related issues)

5. **Angela D. Marconi**, P.E., Engineer, DNREC Division of Air Quality (operations at the Refinery; DNREC monitoring of operations at the Refinery; DAQ involvement in CZA permit request process and related air permit request; and related issues)

6. **David S. Small**, Secretary, DNREC (operations at the Refinery; DNREC monitoring of operations at the Refinery; CZA permit process; DCRC CZA permit application and process; the Secretary's Order and Permit; and related issues)

7. **Kara S. Coats**, Deputy Secretary, DNREC (operations at the Refinery; DNREC monitoring of operations at the Refinery; CZA permit process; DCRC CZA permit application and process; the Secretary's Order and Permit; and related issues)

8. **Ali Mirzakhalili, P.E.**, Division Director, DNREC Division of Air Quality (Delaware City Environmental Coalition March 2012 report; air quality monitoring; and related issues).

10. ***In Limine* Motions**

DCRC and DNREC each submitted to the Board written requests in the form of motions *in limine* to limit/exclude certain testimony, exhibits, affidavits, and/or other evidence sought to be introduced by Appellants. Appellants submitted to the Board responses to DCRC's and DNREC's requests. By email dated February 24, 2017, the Board reported as follows:

> The Chair has decided to deny those requests in their entirety in order to allow the entire Board to hear this evidence, if otherwise admissible, and to give it due weight and consideration should the hearing proceed to the point where such evidence is sought to be introduced by the Appellants. DNREC and DCRC may raise any objections to this evidence at the time it is introduced at the hearing. Please be advised, however, that pursuant to 29 Del.C. § 10125(b), the Chair has the authority to "[e]xclude plainly irrelevant, immaterial, insubstantial, cumulative and privileged evidence" and "limit unduly repetitive proof, rebuttal and cross-examination." The Chair's decision on these requests does not in any way limit this authority with respect to any evidence sought to be introduced by any party during the hearing process.
>
> The Chair has directed that there shall be no further argument or written submissions on this issue.

11. Copies of Exhibits

Each party will provide copies of exhibits to opposing counsel, and deliver ten copies of a bench book of exhibits to the Board at the start of the hearing.

CONCLUDING CERTIFICATION

We hereby certify by the affixing of our signatures to this Joint Final Pre-Hearing Order that it reflects the efforts of all counsel and that we have carefully and completely reviewed all parts of this order prior to its submission to the Board.

/s/ Kenneth T. Kristl
Kenneth T. Kristl, Esq.
Environmental Law Clinic
Delaware Law School
4601 Concord Pike
Wilmington, DE 19803
302-477-2053

Attorney for Appellants Delaware Audubon And League of Women Voters of Delaware

/s/ Joseph C. Schoell
Joseph C. Schoell (I.D. No. 3133)
Drinker, Biddle & Reath LLC
222 Delaware Avenue Suite 1410
Wilmington, DE 19801
(302) 467-4245
Joseph.Schoell@dbr.com

Bart E. Cassidy (admitted pro hoc vice)
Katherine L. Vaccaro (admitted pro hoc vice)
Stephen D. Daly (I.D. No. 6022)
Manko, Gold, Katcher & Fox, LLP
401 City Avenue, Suite 901
Bala Cynwyd, PA 19004
484-430-5700
bcassidy@mankogold.com
kvaccaro@mankogold.com
sdaly@mankogold.com

Attorneys for Intervenor/Appellee Delaware City Refining Company LLC

/s/ Matthew F. Boyer
Max B. Walton (Del. Bar No. 3876)
Matthew F. Boyer (Del. Bar No. 2564)
Lauren P. DeLuca (Del. Bar No. 6024)
CONNOLLY GALLAGHER LLP
The Brandywine Building
1000 North West Street, Suite 1400
Wilmington, DE 19801
302-757-7300

Attorneys for David S. Small, Secretary, and the Delaware Department of Natural Resources and Environmental Control

Entry of the foregoing Joint Final Pre-Hearing Order is hereby APPROVED this 27 day of February, 2017.

Richard Legatski
Chairperson
Delaware Coastal Zone Industrial Control Board

ANNOTATIONS FOR APPEXDIX TAB 6

[1] Identifies the case in which the Stipulation is being made. This is called the "caption of the case," and contains the identity of the court/Board at the top, the party names in an Appellant v. Appellee format, and the case #.

[2] states who is making the Stipulation.

[3] Each paragraph is a single fact. The Stipulation means that both parties agree the Stipulated Fact is true for purposes of the Appeal.

[4] Stipulation signed by the representatives of the parties entering into the Stipulation

NOTE: The document following these annotations is a Joint Pre-Hearing Order entered in an appeal before the CZICB. The document does many things (setting out the parties' positions, the issues that are contested, exhibits, witnesses, and other items), but also includes a set of Stipulated Facts on pages 5 – 10.

Date Received (to be filled In by the Secretary)

Appeal Application Number (to be filled in by the Secretary)

STATE COASTAL ZONE INDUSTRIAL CONTROL BOARD
APPLICATION TO APPEAL FROM
A COASTAL ZONE ACT DECISION

Date

Name of Appellant:

Address and Telephone Number:

A. Identify the Coastal Zone Decision Being Appealed

B. Date of Public Notice of the Coastal Zone Decision________________________________

(to be filled in by the Secretary)

C. Signature of Appellant or Appellant's Representative________________________________

Position or Title (if any)____

D. Briefly State the Reasons for Your Appeal. For example, if you believe the Decision is contrary to the Coastal Zone Act, identify those parts of the law involved and state why the Decision is contrary to them. Your Statement of Reasons for Appeal should be attached to this Application Form.

Please include the appeal fee of One Hundred Dollars ($100) with this Appeal Application. The check or money order should be made out to: **Department of Natural Resources and Environmental Control**

Submit the completed Appeal Application, including the appeal fee, within fourteen (14) days following the public notice of the Coastal Zone Act decision to:

Chair
State Coastal Zone Industrial Control Board
c/o Department of Natural Resources and Environmental Control
89 Kings Highway

Dover, DE 19901

APPENDIX TAB 7

Pre-Hearing Memorandum Example Documents

BEFORE THE ENVIRONMENTAL APPEALS BOARD
OF THE STATE OF DELAWARE

MARTIN LAMPNER, et. al., Appellants, v. DELAWARE DEPARTMENT OF NATURAL RESOURCES AND ENVIRONMENTAL CONTROL, Appellee.	))))))))))))	EAB Docket No. 2019-02

APPELLANTS' PRE-HEARING MEMORANDUM
FOR THE JULY 9, 2019 HEARING

Appellants Martin Lampner, *et al.*, by and through their counsel, hereby file this Pre-Hearing Memorandum to the Board in advance of the July 9, 2019 hearing in this appeal.

This appeal challenges the decision of the DNREC Secretary set forth in Secretary's Order No. 2019-W-0015 dated March 6, 2019 but not publicly noticed until March 20, 2019. The Secretary's Order (Chronology Ex. 12) combines two regulatory decisions: the issuance of a minor marina permit to TAC Beacon 1 LLC pursuant to 7 Del. C. § 6001 *et seq.* and the Marina Regulations, 7 Del. Admin. C. § 7501 *et seq.*, issued thereunder; and (2) the issuance of a subaqueous lands lease to TAC Beacon 1 LLC pursuant to the Subaqueous Lands Act, 7 Del. C. § 6601 *et seq.* and the Regulations Governing The Use of Subaqueous Lands, 7 Del. Admin. C. § 7504 *et seq.*, issued thereunder. The practical effect of the Secretary's Order is that TAC Beacon can build a 10 boat, 2 jet ski marina on Whites Creek in Ocean View, DE as part of a 119-home subdivision known as the Solitudes at White Creek.

TAC Beacon has not appeared or intervened and is not a party to this appeal.

DNREC has stipulated that the Appellants have standing to pursue this appeal.

Appellant's challenge to the Secretary's Order and the approvals therein involves two separate, independent grounds. The first relates to DNREC's failure to give public notice of, the opportunity to comment and/or request a public hearing on, the application upon which the Secretary issued his Order. The second relates to DNREC's failure to consider the regulatory factors that guide the issuance of Marina Permits and Subaqueous Lands Leases. Appellants believe that these failures—whether considered alone or in combination—justify this Board finding that the Secretary's decision was arbitrary, capricious, and/or contrary to law, which requires a remand of both the Marina Permit and the Subaqueous Lands lease back to DNREC.

I. THE SECRETARY'S ORDER AND APPROVALS THEREIN WERE ISSUED WITHOUT COMPLIANCE WITH APPLICABLE STATUTORY AND REGULATORY PROVISIONS REQUIRING PUBLIC NOTICE AND COMMENT.

This appeal challenges a decision with an unusual procedural history. Fortunately, the facts of the history are undisputed.

The underlying administrative process formally began when TAC Beacon submitted its application for the Marina Permit and Subaqueous Lands Lease in November 2016 (Chronology Ex. 1) ("November 2016 Application"). On May 3, 2017, DNREC noticed up a public hearing on the November 2016 Application (Chronology Ex. 4), and in the notice stated that "comments concerning this application should be made in writing to the Division within twenty (20) days from the date of this notice" (i.e., by May 23, 2017). DNREC held the hearing on June 6, 2017 (Chronology Ex. 6 is the transcript of the 6/6/17 Public Hearing). While DNREC allowed public comment at the hearing, the public comment period did not extend beyond that date.

According to the Secretary's Order (at p. 4), subsequent to the public hearing TAC Beacon and DNREC held discussions about revising the marina project. TAC Beacon submitted an Application to DNREC on July 31, 2017 (Chronology Ex. 7) ("July 2017 Application"). As the

Secretary described it in his Order, "[i]t should be noted that the design of this proposed project has been modified significantly by this Applicant from the application originally received by the Department in this matter." Order at p. 2. In short, the July 2017 Application "modified significantly" the design proposed in the November 2016 Application. Despite the admitted significant modification of the project in the July 2017 Application, DNREC has stipulated that it provided no public notice of, opportunity to comment on, or opportunity to request a public hearing about, the July 2017 Application.

Both the Subaqueous Lands Act and the Marina Regulations require that, when DNREC receives an application, it must provide public notice and the opportunity for the public to request a public hearing. *See* 7 Del. C. § 7207(d) (Subaqueous Lands Act);[1] 7 Del. Admin. C. § 7501-4.3.2.4 (Marina Regulations).[2] The Marina Regulations also require that the public be given 45 days to submit public comments on the application. 7 Del. Admin. C. § 7501-4.3.2.4.2. The statute and regulations expressly impose these requirements "upon receipt of an application" and make no exception about, or distinction between, original and revised applications. DNREC received the July 2017 Application, but has stipulated that it did none of the things required by these regulations. Delaware law holds that "once an agency adopts regulations governing how it

---

[1] Upon receipt of an application in proper form, the Secretary shall advertise in a daily newspaper of statewide circulation and in a newspaper of general circulation in the county in which the activity is proposed:

(1) The fact that the application has been received;
(2) A brief description of the nature of the application; and
(3) A statement that a public hearing may be requested by any interested person who offers a meritorious objection to the application.

7 Del. C. § 7207(d).

[2] 4.3.2.4 Public Notice: Upon receipt of an application which is determined to be reasonably complete, the Department will:

4.3.2.4.1 Advertise receipt of the application in two (2) newspapers of statewide circulation.
4.3.2.4.2 Receive public comments for 45 days from the date of notice.
4.3.2.4.3 Allow the applicant to respond to questions posed by the Department and the public within the time period defined for active applications.
4.3.2.4.4 Publish a public notice of the final completed application.
4.3.2.4.5 Receive requests for a public hearing and additional comments for 20 days from the date of notice.

handles its procedures, the agency must follow them. If the agency does not, then the action taken by the agency is invalid." *Hanson v. Delaware State Public Integrity Com'n*, 2012 WL 3860732 (Super. Ct. Aug. 30, 2012), *citing Dugan v. Delaware Harness Racing Commission,* 752 A.2d 529 (Del. 2000); *Mumford & Miller Concrete, Inc. v. Dept of Labor*, 2011 WL 2083940 at *6 (Super. Ct. April 19, 2011) (same). DNREC cannot ignore what its own regulations require.

Appellants suspect that DNREC will try to excuse its failure to satisfy these requirements by raising the faulty argument that, because (in DNREC's mind) the July 2017 Application lessened the impacts of the project as proposed in the November 2016 Application, public notice, comment and opportunity to request a public hearing was unnecessary—i.e., no harm, no foul. This argument fails for four independent reasons. *First*, the language of the Statute and Regulations is mandatory and gives DNREC no discretion over whether or not it needs to comply. *See* 7 Del. C. § 7207(d) ("Secretary ***shall*** . . ."); 7 Del. Admin. C. § 7501-4.3.2.4 ("the Department ***will*** . . .") (emphasis supplied). *Second*, DNREC knew or should have known that Appellants and other public commenters might not agree with DNREC's assessment of how well the July 2017 Application addressed their concerns. In his Order, the Secretary admitted that: (1) "during the public notice periods, [DNREC] received a voluminous amount of written comment against the project," Order at p. 3;[3] (2) the adverse public comment caused DNREC to hold the public hearing, *id.*; and (3) and after notice of the hearing, "over twenty (20) letters of objection to the Applicant's proposed project" were received by DNREC. *Id.* Given this enormous public opposition to the project, it is inexplicable that DNREC would not let the public weigh in on whether the revisions in the July 2017 Application in fact addressed the public's concerns. As nearly every Declaration

[3] According to theTechnical Response Memorandum ("TRM") prepared by DNREC Staff at the request of the Hearing Officer (which is Chronology Exhibit 10), DNREC "received more than 100 written comments against the project" during the public notice period. TRM at p. 2 of 13.

submitted by Appellants (Appellants Exhibit 1) shows, the Appellants wanted to weigh in because they do not believe the July 2017 changes solved their concerns. *Third*, allowing DNREC to avoid its mandatory public notice and comment obligations sets a terrible precedent. It allows an applicant to file an outrageous proposal that the public attacks, and after public comment closes, submit an only slightly less outrageous "revision" that allows DNREC to say "look how much smaller the impact is" without any opportunity for the public to show why the slightly revised proposal is still too outrageous. That reads public notice and comment out of the permitting process.

Fourth, allowing DNREC to shirk its mandatory duties of public notice and comment risks making appeals to this Board a mockery. This Board's Rule 5.3 includes language that "Appellants other than permit applicants or an alleged violator ***may only introduce evidence which was before the Secretary***" (emphasis supplied). To the extent the Board believes this Rule should apply and be enforced as written,[4] DNREC's actions here may severely limit the scope of what Appellants may be able to present to the Board. Why? Because DNREC's failure to meet its mandatory notice, comment, and public hearing duties *means that Appellants never had (and indeed were actively denied) the opportunity to put* ***anything*** *before the Secretary on the particulars of the July 2017 Application.* It would be patently unfair (and likely an unconstitutional denial of due process) if the Board were to prevent Appellants from presenting evidence on what happens under the July 2017 Application because that evidence was not (and—thanks to DNREC—could not have been) put before the Secretary. If the Board wants to enforce Rule 5.3, it must reverse and remand so that the appropriate public notice and opportunity to comment be given, and Appellants have the

[4] For the record, Appellants disagree with the limitations imposed by this language, and reserve the right to challenge it if needed.

chance to put information about the Revised Application before the Secretary so that the record can be complete. Otherwise, Appellants' right to appeal is rendered virtually meaningless.[5]

For these reasons, DNREC's failure to perform its mandatory duties to give public notice, the opportunity to comment, and the opportunity to request a public hearing on the Revised Application provides an independent basis for the Board to find the Secretary and DNREC acted arbitrarily, capriciously, and contrary to law.[6] The Board should therefore reverse the Secretary's Order, and the Marina Permit and Subaqueous Lands Lease approved therein, and remand them back to the Secretary and DNREC.

II. THE SECRETARY'S ORDER, AND THE APPROVALS CONTAINED THEREIN, WERE ISSUED WITHOUT COMPLIANCE WITH APPLICABLE STATUTORY AND REGULATORY PROVISIONS.

The statutory and regulatory provisions governing Subaqueous Lands Leases and Marina Permits impose a variety of requirements on DNREC before issuing such permits or leases.

The "Purposes" section at the beginning of Regulations Governing the Use of Subaqueous Lands, 7 Del. Admin. § 7504 *et seq*., echoes the Subaqueous Lands Act, 7 Del. C. § 7201, in stating that "subaqueous lands within the boundaries of Delaware constitute an important resource of the State" and that the Secretary is empowered to regulate them "in order to protect the public interest." These Regulations therefore impose numerous requirements on how the Secretary and DNREC go about granting leases of subaqueous lands like the Secretary did to TAC Beacon. Among the biggest of those requirements are: 7 Del. Admin. C. §§ **7504-4.2**;[7] **7504-4.6**, which states "[t]he

---

[5] Or, the Board could decide that Rule 5.3's limits on what Appellants can present no longer apply. That would resolve this fourth argument, but would do nothing on the first three arguments presented here.

[6] Because this argument raises a pure question of law (given that there is no dispute about the facts), the Board could take up this issue at the beginning of the hearing and, if it decides that remand back to the Secretary is appropriate, avoid having to get into the merits of this appeal.

[7] Section 7504-4.2 states: An application may be denied if the activity could cause harm to the environment, either singly or in combination with other activities or existing conditions, which cannot be mitigated sufficiently."

Department shall consider the public interest in any proposed activity which might affect the use of subaqueous lands," and lists nine specific considerations, including "the potential effect on the public with respect to commerce, navigation, recreation, aesthetic enjoyment, natural resources, and other uses of the subaqueous lands" (§ 7504-4.6.3) and "the extent to which the applicant's primary objectives and purposes can be realized without the use of such lands (avoidance)" (§ 7504-4.6.5); and **7504-4.7** ("The Department shall consider the impact on the environment" with 15 different topics listed).

The Marina Regulations, 7 Del. Admin. § 7501 *et seq.*, likewise articulate numerous requirements for the Secretary and DNREC when issuing marina permits. Among the biggest of those requirements are: **§§ 7201-11.2**, which sets forth the process and criteria by which the Department must review a marina permit application, including that "the Department will also consider the public interest in any activity which might affect the use of subaqueous lands;" **7201-11.2.3**, which involves considering, among other things, "the potential effect on the public with respect to commerce, navigation, recreation, aesthetic enjoyment, natural resources, and other uses of the subaqueous lands" (§ 7201-11.2.3.1); **7201-11.3**, entitled "Environmental Siting Considerations," which states that "The Department's Review of all permit applications will include consideration of the following" and then goes on to list ten different categories of considerations, including impacts on water quality, wetlands, and cumulative impacts; and **7201-11.4** entitled "Planning and Design Requirements," which includes consideration of navigation and access channels (§ 7201-11.4.4) and vessel traffic and navigation (§ 7201-11.4.5) ("marinas shall be designed to minimize adverse effects on the existing public and private use of waters of the State," § 7201-11.4.5.1).

Appellants believe the evidence will show that these regulatory requirements were not followed with respect to the TAC Beacon marina. The Board will hear evidence about the adverse impacts on navigation and the environment, the inadequate design of the marina that worsens these impacts, and how the marina is not needed. From the public use and interest perspective that the Secretary and DNREC are required to follow, the granting of the Marina Permit and Subaqueous Lands Lease in the Secretary's Order was arbitrary, capricious, and contrary to law. The Board should therefore reverse the Secretary's Order, and the Marina Permit and Subaqueous Lands Lease approved therein, and either deny them entirely or remand them back to the Secretary and DNREC.

Respectfully submitted,

July 3, 2019

/s/ Kenneth T. Kristl

Kenneth T. Kristl, Esq. (DE Bar No. 5200)
Delaware Law School
Environmental & Natural Resources Law Clinic
4601 Concord Pike
Wilmington, DE 19803
(302) 477-2053
ktkristl@widener.edu

Counsel for Appellants

CERTIFICATE OF SERVICE

Kenneth T. Kristl, an attorney, hereby certifies that he served a copy of the foregoing **APPELLANTS' PRE-HEARING MEMORANDUM FOR THE JULY 9, 2019 HEARING** upon:

Kayli Spialter, Esq.
Deputy Attorney General, Environmental Unit
Delaware Department of Justice
820 North French Street
Wilmington, DE 19801
Counsel for DNREC

By electronic mail on July 3, 2019.

___/s/ Kenneth T. Kristl____________
Kenneth T. Kristl, Esq. (DE Bar No. 5200)
Delaware Law School
Environmental & Natural Resources Law Clinic
4601 Concord Pike
Wilmington, DE 19803
(302) 477-2053
ktkristl@widener.edu

Counsel for Appellants

BEFORE THE COASTAL ZONE INDUSTRIAL CONTROL BOARD

DELAWARE AUDUBON and LEAGUE OF WOMEN VOTERS OF DELAWARE, Appellants, v. DELAWARE DEPARTMENT OF NATURAL RESOURCES AND ENVIRONMENTAL CONTROL and DELAWARE CITY REFINERY CO., LLC, Appellees.	)	No. 2017-01 Appeal of Secretary's Order No. 2015-CZ-0050 and Coastal Zone Act Permit 427P

APPELLANTS'S PRE-HEARING MEMO/ STATEMENT OF LEGAL ISSUES

In order to assist the Board in preparing for the hearing in this appeal, Appellants Delaware Audubon Society and League of Women Voters of Delaware (collectively, "Appellants") hereby submit this Pre-Hearing Memo setting forth their Statement of the Legal Issues raised by this appeal.

In this appeal, Appellants challenge the Secretary of the Delaware Department of Natural Resources and Environmental Control's Order 2016-CZ-0050, issued December 27, 2016 and publicly noticed January 1, 2017 (Order), which grants Delaware City Refinery Company, LLC Coastal Zone Act Permit No. 427P (Permit). The Permit allows the receipt and transshipment of up to 10,000 barrels per day of ethanol from DCRC's facility located at 4550 Wrangle Hill Road, Delaware City, New Castle County (Refinery). Appellants ask the Board to reverse the Order and deny Coastal Zone Act Permit No. 427P for one or more of seven reasons listed in the Statement of Appeal.

In order for the Board to better understand the seven legal grounds for this appeal, Appellants believe it is helpful to first articulate some fundamental facts and law that underlie this appeal.

Fundamental Facts Underlying The Appeal

Appellants believe there are four fundamental sets of facts that are important to framing the issues in this appeal. Appellants believe that the evidence will show each of the following facts to be true:

1. The Refinery does not manufacture ethanol[1]; thus, the ethanol that will be shipped pursuant to the Permit must be shipped to the Refinery. The Refinery indicated in its Application for the Permit that it "received and continues to receive ethanol," Application p. 6—a process that would be wholly unnecessary if the Refinery manufactured ethanol itself. Nor has the Refinery ever identified the ethanol it plans to ship as one of the products produced at the Refinery. Thus, the ethanol that is the subject of the Permit will be shipped to the Refinery from a manufacturer located somewhere else.

2. The ethanol being shipped pursuant to the Permit will arrive at the Refinery in whole or in part by rail. In its Application, the Refinery stated that it receives ethanol "via marine vessels at the pier or by rail" (Application, p. 6). As the Board knows from the 2013 proceedings before it concerning the Refinery's Marine Vapor Recovery System air permit, the Refinery utilizes rail facilities—sometimes referred to as the "Double Rail Loop"—that were built in 2011. At the public hearing on the Permit, Refinery representative Larry Boyd, senior environmental engineer, stated when testifying about the project's background and objectives: "The refinery has an existing rail unloading facility that is going to be repurposed. It has been

[1] The ethanol that is the subject matter of the Permit is sometimes referred to as "denatured ethanol," which is ethanol with gasoline additives in it. Because the Order refers to the substance as "ethanol," Appellants do so here.

repurposed to denatured ethanol service from crude service." 10/26/16 Public Hearing Transcript, p. 9 (lines 15-19). PBF Energy, the owner of the Refinery, has publicly touted that, as part of its "Commercial Optimization" strategy, it plans to be "importing and distributing ethanol on the East Coast at its Delaware City rail facilities." PBF Energy, Inc. presentation at Barclays CEO Energy Power Conference September 2016 p. 9.

3. **The ethanol being shipped pursuant to the Permit will not be processed in the Refinery; in other words, the Permit allows the transshipment of ethanol.** The Refinery's Application for the Permit indicates that the Refinery uses ethanol it receives "to blend with gasoline at the Marketing Terminal's truck loading rack to meet the Renewable Fuel Standard program's requirements." Application, p. 6; *see* Boyd, 10/26/16 Transcript, p. 10 (lines 7-10). While neither the Application nor the Refinery presentation at the public hearing quantified the amount of ethanol used by the Refinery for such gasoline blending, internal DNREC emails suggest that the Refinery's own blending efforts use about 2,000 barrels/day (bpd) of ethanol. *See* 3/11/16 email from Ravi Rangan to Phillip Cherry, Ali Mirzakhalili, Kevin Coyle with Cc: to Paul Foster Re: DCRC EtOH Project; 6/9/16 email from Ravi Rangan to Phillip Cherry, Kara Coats, Marjorie Crofts, Valarie Edge, Patrice Emory, James Faedtke, Paul Foster, Virgil Holmes, Ali Mirzakhalili, Caol Riggs, David Small, with Cc: to Penny Gentry, Angela Marconi, Lindsay Rennie Re: DCRC Permitting Projects. With the Permit allowing the Refinery to ship 10,000 bpd of ethanol (which is **five times more** than the Refinery's daily needs), the 10,000 bpd will be brought to the Refinery, put in a storage tank, and then simply shipped out on the marine barges without any processing of those 10,000 bpd by the Refinery. Indeed, that is consistent with PBF Energy's publicly stated strategy to be simply "importing and distributing ethanol on the East Coast." This process of receiving then simply shipping out a

product without processing is sometimes referred to as "transshipment"—and that is exactly what the Permit allows the Refinery to do.

4. **The Refinery did not handle or use ethanol until 2006.** As noted above, the Refinery's Application explains that it received ethanol for blending with gasoline "to meet the Renewable Fuel Standard program's requirements," Application, p. 6—requirements that were created by EPA's Renewable Fuel Standard program to meet the mandates of the federal Energy Policy Act of 2005. *Id.* As a result, the Refinery did not start receiving ethanol for its own blending uses until 2006. *See* Boyd, 10/26/16 Public Hearing Transcript, p. 10 (lines 10-11) ("We have been receiving the ethanol by barge since 2006 at the refinery"); 12/22/05 Application for Coastal Zone Act Status Decision by Premcor Refining Group, Inc. concerning switch from methyl tertiary butyl ether (MTBE) to ethanol as gasoline blending component.

Fundamental Legal Principles Underlying This Appeal

In addition to the fundamental facts set forth above, there are important and fundamental legal principles central to the resolution of the issues raised in this appeal. Appellants believe it is important to first identify and articulate those principles in a general way.[2]

1. **New Bulk Product Transfer Facilities Are Prohibited Under the Act.** In § 7001, the Coastal Zone Act explicitly states as part of the purpose behind the Act:

> It is further determined that offshore bulk product transfer facilities represent a significant danger of pollution to the coastal zone and generate pressure for the construction of industrial plants in the coastal zone, which construction is declared to be against public policy. **For these reasons, prohibition against bulk product transfer facilities in the coastal zone is deemed imperative.**

7 Del. C. § 7001 (emphasis supplied). As a result, § 7003 of the Act specifically prohibits new bulk product transfer facilities:

[2] To assist the Board in understanding the legal requirements at issue here, Appellants are submitting an Appendix to this Pre-Hearing Memo that contains the relevant statutory and regulatory provisions as well as two decisions cited later in this Memo.

> Heavy industry uses of any kind not in operation on June 28, 1971, are prohibited in the coastal zone and no permits may be issued therefor. **In addition, offshore gas, liquid or solid bulk product transfer facilities which are not in operation on June 28, 1971, are prohibited in the coastal zone, and no permit may be issued therefor.**

7 Del. C. § 7003 (emphasis supplied). The Act defines a bulk product transfer facility as follows:

> "Bulk product transfer facility" means any port or dock facility, whether an artificial island or attached to shore by any means, for the transfer of bulk quantities of any substance from vessel to onshore facility or vice versa. Not included in this definition is a docking facility or pier for a single industrial or manufacturing facility for which a permit is granted or which is a nonconforming use. Likewise, docking facilities for the Port of Wilmington are not included in this definition.

7 Del. C. § 7002(f). Thus, a docking facility for the transfer of bulk quantities of any substance from shore to ship that was (1) not engaged in that activity on June 28, 1971, and/or (2) not used for a single industrial or manufacturing facility, is prohibited under § 7003 of the Act. As will be made clear in their arguments concerning several of the Grounds for Appeal below, Appellants believe that the transshipment of ethanol allowed under the Permit violates these provisions of the Act and the regulations issued thereunder.

2. Under the Act and its Regulations, Nonconforming Uses can operate and may expand, but the right to expand is not absolute. While the Act generally prohibits new heavy industry and bulk product transfer facilities, it treats pre-existing facilities somewhat differently. In 7 Del. C. § 7002(b), the Act recognizes a third category called "nonconforming use" and defines it as follows:

> "Nonconforming use" means a use, whether of land or of a structure, which does not comply with the applicable use provisions in this chapter where such use was lawfully in existence and in active use prior to June 28, 1971.

The Refinery—whose refining operations fit the definition of "heavy industry" but were in existence and active use on June 28, 1971—is a nonconforming use under the Act.

The prohibitions in § 7003 apply to heavy industry and bulk product transfer facilities "not in operation on June 28, 1971"—in other words, which are not a nonconforming use. 7 Del. C. § 7004(a), the permitting section of the CZA, reaffirms this conclusion: "Any nonconforming use in existence and in active use on June 28, 1971, shall not be prohibited by this chapter." Thus, the Act allows nonconforming uses to continue to operate in their original state.

In addition, the Act allows nonconforming uses to expand:

> Any nonconforming use in existence and in active use on June 28, 1971, shall not be prohibited by this chapter and all expansion or extension of nonconforming uses, as defined herein, and all expansion or extension of uses for which a permit is issued pursuant to this chapter, are likewise allowed only by permit.

7 Del. C. § 7004(a). However, the right to expand is not absolute, and in fact is subject to two important and independent legal constraints.

The first independent legal constraint is found in the statutory and regulatory provisions flatly prohibiting certain new uses. As noted above, § 7003 prohibits new heavy industry uses and bulk product transfer facilities that were "not in operation on June 28, 1971" and provides that "no permit may be issued therefor." Thus, an applicant seeking to build a brand new facility that is a new heavy industry use or bulk product transfer facility cannot obtain a permit for such a prohibited use because "no permit may be issued therefor." As explained below, § 7003's language prohibiting permits for a new heavy industry use or bulk product transfer facility must apply to the permit that a nonconforming use must obtain under § 7004(a) for an expansion. In addition, the CZA Regulations expressly declare that "the following uses or activities are prohibited in the Coastal Zone," 7 Del. Admin. 101 ("CZA Regulations") at § 4.0, with 9 different prohibited uses or activities listed. CZA Regulations §§ 4.1-4.9. These "Section 4

Prohibitions" clearly limit the ability of a nonconforming use to expand to do one of the 9 listed prohibited activities. Thus, for example, a nonconforming bulk product transfer operation could not expand to start a new heavy industry use because CZA Regulations § 4.1 flatly prohibits "Heavy industry use of any kind not in operation on June 28, 1971." Likewise, a nonconforming heavy industry use could not expand to begin a new bulk product transfer facility because CZA Regulation § 4.5 flatly prohibits "Bulk product transfer facilities and pipelines which serve as bulk transfer facilities that were not in operation on June 28, 1971."

The second independent legal constraint is found in the requirements related to applying for and obtaining a Coastal Zone Act Permit. These requirements, found in 7 Del. C. § 7004(b) and supplemented by the requirements in CZA Regulations §§ 8.1 – 10.4, mean that a nonconforming use seeking to expand must first satisfy important substantive and procedural provisions before an expansion can occur.

3. **The Secretary's Claim that Nonconforming Uses May Expand Simply by Obtaining a Coastal Zone Act Permit Fundamentally Misstates the Law.** The core issue in this appeal is the Coastal Zone Act status of the transshipment of ethanol allowed under the Permit. Appellants contend that the transshipment is best characterized as a new bulk product transfer facility not in operation on June 28, 1971 and therefore prohibited by 7 Del. C. § 7003 and §§ 4.5 – 4.6 of the CZA Regulations[3] and/or an expansion of the Refinery's heavy industry use beyond its Appendix B footprint and therefore prohibited by § 7003 and § 4.2 of the CZA Regulations.[4] The Secretary viewed the transshipment as an expansion of the Refinery's nonconforming use, and the Order and decision to issue the Permit apparently rests on the legal view that *any* expansion of a nonconforming use is permissible so long as the Secretary issues a

[3] The factual and legal bases for this argument are discussed in Appeal Grounds #2 and 3 below.
[4] The factual and legal bases for this argument are discussed in Appeal Ground #1 below.

permit under 7 Del. C. § 7004. This legal view rests on an overly broad and fundamentally flawed view of what nonconforming uses can do under the law.

Initially, it is important to note that Secretary's view that *any* expansion of a nonconforming use is allowable by CZA permit conflicts with the statutory provisions of the Act. The ability of a nonconforming use to expand is subject to the legal constraints created by the flat prohibitions in 7 Del. C. § 7003 and §§ 4.0 – 4.9 of the CZA Regulations. As § 7003 puts it, "no permit may be issued" for what amounts to a heavy industry use or bulk product transfer facility that was not in operation on June 28, 1971. The language is absolute; no exception to these prohibitions for expansions by nonconforming uses is included in §§ 7003 or 7004. This is reinforced by the Section 4 Prohibitions in the CZA Regulations. Thus, nonconforming uses cannot expand in *any* way provided they get a permit; rather, they can only expand (and therefore get permits) in ways that do not trigger these statutory and regulatory prohibitions.

Three important principles of statutory interpretation buttress this conclusion. First, when a statute as a whole is unambiguous, there is no reasonable doubt as to the meaning of the words used and the interpretation of the statute "is then limited to an application of the literal meaning of the words." *Coastal Barge Corp. v. Coastal Zone Indus. Control Bd.*, 492 A.2d 1242, 1246 (Del. 1985). The literal meaning of § 7003 is that "no permit may be issued" for what amounts to a new heavy industry or bulk product transfer facility—including a permit for a nonconforming use expansion. Second, the permitting power in 7 Del. C. § 7004(a) cannot be read in isolation from § 7003; rather, "each part or section should be read in light of every other part or section to produce an harmonious whole," *Coastal Barge*, 482 A.2d at 1245. The most harmonious reading of these sections together is that nonconforming uses can expand by permit, but cannot expand to engage in the activities prohibited by 7 Del. C. § 7003 of new heavy industry or bulk product transfer facilities. Finally, when interpreting a statute, "the fundamental rule is to ascertain and give effect to the intent of the legislature." *Id.* The clear intent of the Act is set forth in 7 Del. C. § 7001:

> It is hereby determined that the coastal areas of Delaware are the most critical areas for the future of the State in terms of the quality of life in the State. It is, therefore, the declared public policy of the State to control the location, extent and type of industrial development in Delaware's coastal areas. In so doing, the State can better protect the natural environment of its bay and coastal areas and safeguard their use primarily for recreation and tourism. Specifically, this chapter seeks to prohibit entirely the construction of new heavy industry in its coastal areas, which industry is determined to be incompatible with the protection of that natural environment in those areas . . . . It is further determined that offshore bulk product transfer facilities represent a significant danger of pollution to the coastal zone and generate pressure for the construction of industrial plants in the coastal zone, which construction is declared to be against public policy. For these reasons, prohibition against bulk product transfer facilities in the coastal zone is deemed imperative.

To allow a nonconforming use to expand by creating a new heavy industry use or bulk product transfer facility under the permit authority of § 7004(a) would be inconsistent with this "strongly worded statutory purpose." *Coastal Barge*, 482 A.2d at 1246. Thus, the Secretary's view that a nonconforming use can expand in *any* way fundamentally misstates the law by ignoring the relevant statutory and regulatory limitations.

Despite this conflict with the Act itself, the Order cites three sources of legal support for the Secretary's broad view of nonconforming use expansions: § 6.3 of the CZA Regulations, § 1.2 of the DNREC Guidance found at Appendix C to the CZA Regulations; and language from *Kearney v. Coastal Zone Indus. Control Bd.*, 2005 WL 3844219, *5-6 (Del. Super. Ct. March 18, 2005), *aff'd*, 897 A.2d 767 (Table) (Del. 2006). Order at 3-4. None of these sources in fact support the overly broad interpretation offered by the Secretary.

§ 6.3 of the CZA Regulations Does *Not Support the Secretary's Broad View* – Section 6.3 of the CZA Regulations appears within Section 6.0 as part of a list (§§ 6.1 – 6.3) of "uses or activities [which] are permissible in the Coastal Zone by permit." CZA Regulations, § 6.0. Section 6.3 identifies as one of these permissible uses the following:

> Any new activity, with the exception of those listed in Section 5.0 of these regulations proposed to be initiated after promulgation of these regulations by an existing heavy industry or a new or existing manufacturing facility that may result in any negative impact on the following factors as found in 7 Del.C. §7004 (b) . . .

There are at least two reasons why this language does not support the Secretary's claim that nonconforming uses can expand to undertake any activity upon receipt of a Coastal Zone Act Permit. *First*, the language of § 6.3 does not refer to nonconforming uses at all; instead, it only cites "existing heavy industry" and "new or existing manufacturing facilities." On its face, it does not cover nonconforming bulk product transfer facilities; thus, it cannot be read to allow expansions of such nonconforming uses. This is important to this appeal because it means that at best only the Refinery's nonconforming heavy industry use would qualify under § 6.3; even if the Refinery could somehow claim status as a nonconforming bulk product transfer facility (a factual issue Appellants would vigorously dispute), § 6.3 could not apply to allow its expansion.

Second, and more fundamentally, § 6.3 cannot be read in isolation. Section 6 of the CZA Regulations (uses allowable by permit) are one part of a three-part structure set up in the CZA Regulations, along with the Section 4 Prohibitions and the "uses not regulated" listed in Section 5. Thus, § 6.3 must be read in conjunction with the Section 4 Prohibitions; the "new activity" covered by § 6.3 cannot include one of the 9 prohibited uses or activities in §§ 4.1 – 4.9 lest the Section 4 prohibitions are rendered meaningless and superfluous. Indeed, the absurdity of the Secretary's position is found in the following simple analysis: if § 6.3's "any new activity" really means that an "existing" (i.e., nonconforming) heavy industry can expand to do *anything* it wants, then that would include the ability to expand in size to as large as it wants. Yet § 4.2 of the CZA Regulations, which prohibits "expansions of any non-conforming uses beyond their footprints as depicted in Appendix B of these regulations," would be rendered absolutely meaningless, given that it can only apply in the situation of an expansion of a nonconforming use. As with statutes, *see Coastal Barge*, 492 A.2d at 1245, regulations should not be interpreted in ways which render other regulatory provisions meaningless or "surplusage," but instead should be "read in light of every other part or section to produce an harmonious whole." *Garrison v. Red Clay School Dist.*, 3 A.3d 264, 267 (Del. 2010). The only way to harmonize §§ 4.2 and 6.3 and give meaning to both sections is to interpret § 6.3 as allowing any new activity by an "existing" (i.e., nonconforming) heavy industry or new or existing manufacturing facility to be subject to potential permitting under the Act *so long as it is not prohibited under Section 4*. Thus, § 6.3 does not support the Secretary's overly-broad reading, but instead subjects a nonconforming use's expansion by permit to the prohibitions in Section 4.[5]

§ 1.2 of the DNREC Guidance found at Appendix C to the CZA Regulations Does Not Support the Secretary's Broad View – The Order cites several times to §§ 1.1 and/or 1.2 of the DNREC Guidance found at Appendix C to the CZA Regulations. Section 1.1 characterizes the CZA Regulations as being "designed to ensure environmental improvement in the Coastal Zone while at the same time providing industry with the needed flexibility to remain competitive in a global marketplace." Section 1.2 then states:

[5] And, as Grounds # 1-3 below make clear, Appellants believe that the transshipment of ethanol under the Permit violates §§ 4.2, 4.5, and 4.6 of the CZA Regulations.

> In order to meet these two goals, a regulatory process comprised of regulatory exemptions, permitting requirements and offset provisions has been developed. This regulatory process has been designed so that each nonconforming use and new manufacturing uses can add new products, change existing products, increase production capacity, add new processes and modify existing processes or do any other activity so long as these activities are: 1) undertaken in a way that assures environmental improvement in the Coastal Zone; and 2) undertaken in such a way that they meet the six criteria outlined in the Coastal Zone Act.

This language suggests—much more explicitly than § 6.3 of the CZA Regulations does—that nonconforming uses can do *any* activity (including expansions that add new products and processes or increase production capacity) simply by meeting the permitting requirements of the Act—exactly the legal view the Secretary adopts in the Order. However, the language of § 1.2 does not in fact support the Secretary's position for at least 2 reasons.

First, as the caption at the beginning of Appendix C makes clear, this is DNREC "guidance." As § 1.4 of Appendix C explicitly states: "**This guidance is, however, not a regulation and does not have the force of law**" (emphasis supplied). Thus, citation to the language in § 1.2 is not binding on this Board.

Second, after expressly stating that the DNREC guidance found in Appendix C is not regulation and lacks the force of law, § 1.4 of Appendix C goes on to explicitly state: "**In the event of a conflict between this guidance and the regulations, the regulations will prevail**" (emphasis supplied). As noted above, the Section 4 Prohibitions flatly bar any of the nine listed actions in Section 4; thus, to the extent that § 1.2's language allowing *any* activity by a nonconforming use includes activities that fall within one or more of the Section 4 Prohibitions, the Section 4 Prohibition controls and the language of § 1.2 of Appendix C must give way. Thus—as was the case with § 6.3 of the CZA Regulations—the language of § 1.2 must be read as allowing activity that is not prohibited by § 7003 or any one of the nine subsections of Section 4 of the CZA Regulations. Section 1.2 of Appendix C does not support the Secretary's overly-broad reading that *any* expansion of a nonconforming use is allowable by permit under the Act.

The Kearney Case Does Not Support the Secretary's Broad View – The final support for the Secretary's view that *any* expansion of a nonconforming use is allowable by permit is citation to language in *Kearney v. Coastal Zone Indus. Control Bd.*, 2005 WL 3844219, *5-6 (Del. Super. Ct. March 18, 2005), *aff'd*, 897 A.2d 767 (Table) (Del. 2006). Order at 4. In fact, *Kearney* offers no such valid legal support.

Kearney involved an appeal of a Coastal Zone Act permit issued to DuPont that allowed the construction and operation of a new Spent Acid Recovery ((SAR) plant within the footprint of the Refinery after the old unit was destroyed in a catastrophic accident. 2005 WL 3844219, *1. This Board affirmed the issuance of the permit, and Kearney appealed. In response to Kearney's argument that the Act is merely a zoning act, and thus nonconforming uses should never be allowed to expand because they must "wither and die," the Court stated the following:

> Even if Mr. Kearney's characterization of zoning is correct in a general sense, it ignores the plain language of the Act. Section 7004(a) of the Act provides that "all expansion or extension of nonconforming uses, as defined herein, and all expansion or extension of uses for which a permit is issued pursuant to this chapter, are likewise allowed only by permit." Subsection (b) provides that, when the Secretary makes a permitting decision, he must consider, "Economic effect, including the number of jobs created and the income which will be generated by the wages and salaries of these jobs in relation to the amount of land required, and the amount of tax revenue potentially accruing to state and local government."
>
> This language makes it clear that the General Assembly did not intend to doom every existing, non-conforming use in the coastal zone to extinction by attrition. Instead, the legislature clearly expects the Secretary to make a judgment call on any proposed expansions, balancing environmental and economic factors to reach the best result for Delaware and its citizens.

> The reason for writing the Act this way is obvious. At issue is not a bar or junkyard whose loss would go unnoticed; it is a massive refinery directly or indirectly employing hundreds of people and providing millions of dollars in state tax revenues. Deciding to close it down by disallowing all competitive expansion, particularly expansion that lessens its pollution output, without considering all relevant factors, would contravene legislative intent.

Id. at *5-6. Thus, what the Court was responding to was an argument which claimed that nonconforming uses can **never** expand under the Act because they are supposed to "wither and die," and the Court responded by pointing out that the language of § 7004(a) in fact allows expansions by permit. What the Court did **not** do—because the issue was not before it—was decide that **any** and **every** type of nonconforming use expansion is allowable by permit. Nor did the Court decide—again because the issue was not before it—whether nonconforming use expansions by permit are limited by the express Section 4 Prohibitions in the CZA Regulations. In short, the Court found that **some** nonconforming use expansions are possible because § 7004(a) expressly says so, and the language about the General Assembly's expectations and intent supports this conclusion. What the Court **did not do**—again, because the issue was not before the Court given the "wither or die" argument it was deciding—was to define the complete scope of the expansions allowed. Thus, *Kearney* does not support the Secretary's view that any expansion of a nonconforming use is permissible upon issuance of a permit because the Court never decided that issue.

With these fundamental facts and legal principles as starting points, Appellants respectfully suggest that the Secretary, when he issued the Order and Permit, erred as a matter of law and fact in seven different ways. Appellants discuss each of these seven grounds for appeal in turn.

I. APPEAL GROUND #1: THE ORDER AND PERMIT VIOLATE 7 DEL. C. § 7003 AND SECTION 4.2 OF THE CZA REGULATIONS BECAUSE THAT PORTION OF THE DOCKING FACILITY USED TO RECEIVE THE ETHANOL IS OUTSIDE THE FOOTPRINT OF THE REFINERY'S NONCONFORMING USE AS SET FORTH IN APPENDIX B TO THE CZA REGULATIONS.

One of the nine Section 4 Prohibitions in the CZA Regulations is found in § 4.2, which prohibits the following use or activity in the Coastal Zone: "Expansion of any non-conforming uses beyond their footprint(s) as depicted in Appendix B of these regulations." The CZA Regulations define "footprint" as follows:

> **"Footprint"** means the geographical extent of non-conforming uses as they existed on June 28, 1971 as depicted in Appendix B.

CZA Regulations, § 3.0. Appendix B consists of a series of aerial-type photographs of various nonconforming uses with lines depicting the boundaries of each nonconforming use. In fact, there is an Appendix B photograph for the Refinery (although it is captioned "Star Enterprise" because that was the name of a prior owner/operator of the Refinery). Note that the definition of "footprint" is purely one of geography; thus, § 4.2's prohibition is violated whenever a nonconforming use goes beyond the line in the Appendix B photograph ***regardless of the use to which the area beyond the line is put.***

Appellants believe that the evidence will show that the Double Rail Loop facility by which the Refinery will receive ethanol for transshipment under the Permit is located outside the Appendix B footprint for the Refinery.[6] As such, the Refinery is in violation of § 4.2, and thus in

[6] While mere geographic exceedance of the Appendix B footprint lines is sufficient to violate § 4.2, is it also important to note that the Double Rail Loop is part of the "docking facility" involved in transshipping ethanol. The CZA Regulations define "docking Facility" in this way:

> "**Docking Facility**" means any structures and/or equipment used to temporarily secure a vessel to a shoreline or another vessel so that materials, cargo, and/or people may be transferred between the vessel and the shore, or between two vessels together with associated land, equipment, and structures so as to allow the receiving, accumulating, safekeeping, storage, and preparation of cargoes for further shipment, and administrative maintenance purposes directly related to such receiving, accumulating, safekeeping, storage, and preparation of cargoes for further shipment.

violation of the prohibitions in 7 Del. C. § 7003. The Order and Permit, by allowing the use of an area prohibited by the CZA Regulations and the Act to import ethanol, is therefore contrary to law. The Board should therefore reverse the Order and deny the Permit.

II. APPEAL GROUND #2: THE ORDER AND PERMIT VIOLATE 7 DEL. C. § 7003 AND SECTION 4.5 OF THE CZA REGULATIONS BECAUSE THEY ALLOW A BULK PRODUCT TRANSFER FACILITY THAT WAS NOT IN OPERATION ON JUNE 28, 1971.

As noted in the discussion of fundamental legal concepts above, 7 Del. C. § 7003 provides that "offshore gas, liquid or solid bulk product transfer facilities which are not in operation on June 28, 1971, are prohibited in the coastal zone, and no permit may be issued therefor." Section 4.5 of the CZA Regulations likewise identifies as one of the Section 4 Prohibitions "bulk product transfer facilities . . . that were not in operation on June 28, 1971" as one of the nine "uses or activities [] prohibited in the Coastal Zone."

Appellants believe that the evidence will show that the proposed transshipment of ethanol allowed under the Permit is in fact a bulk product transfer facility that was not in operation on June 28, 1971, and therefore is not allowed under 7 Del. C. § 7003 and § 4.5 of the CZA Regulations. The fact that the Refinery did not handle ethanol until 2006 means that it could not possibly have been engaging in such shipments on June 28, 1971.[7] As such, the Order and Permit were issued contrary to law. The Board should therefore reverse the Order and deny the Permit.

CZA Regulations § 3.0. Thus, "Docking Facility" includes not just the dock or pier **but also** the "associated land, equipment, and structures so as to allow the receiving, accumulating, safekeeping, storage, and preparation of cargoes for further shipment . . . ." The Double Rail Look at which ethanol will arrive at the Refinery plays an essential role in the "receiving, accumulating, safekeeping, storage and preparation" of the ethanol for shipment under the Permit—indeed, without it, there are no shipments of ethanol from the Refinery's dock.

[7] Likewise, the independent fact that the Double Rail Loop portion of the "docking facility" being used in the transshipment of ethanol was not built until 2011 means that the docking facility was not "in operation" on June 28, 1971, and is therefore "new" and subject to 7 Del. C. § 7003 and § 4.5 of the CZA Regulations.

The Order, while expressly acknowledging that the Refinery "has not demonstrated that the storing and shipment of ethanol to or from the refinery's docking facility by barge was occurring in 1971 so as to be within its initial nonconforming use," Order at 5, nevertheless concluded that the transshipment of ethanol would not be a new bulk product transfer facility. Id. at 5-6.[8] In reaching this conclusion, the Secretary relies upon the definition of bulk product transfer facility found in 7 Del. C § 7002(f),[9] which states:

> "Bulk product transfer facility" means any port or dock facility, whether an artificial island or attached to shore by any means, for the transfer of bulk quantities of any substance from vessel to onshore facility or vice versa. Not included in this definition is a docking facility or pier for a single industrial or manufacturing facility for which a permit is granted or which is a nonconforming use. Likewise, docking facilities for the Port of Wilmington are not included in this definition.

The Secretary points to the "nonconforming use" language in the second sentence's exclusion and claims that "the integrated docking facility at the refinery is not a prohibited bulk product transfer facility but rather is a legally existing nonconforming use." Order at 6. The Secretary concludes that the integrated docking facility is a "use for which a permit may be granted" because "section 7004 specifically permits the expansion and extension of nonconforming uses so long as certain statutory criteria, designed to result in environmental improvements, are met." *Id.* The Secretary's legal analysis is wrong for several reasons.

Initially, it is important to note that, as explained in the Fundamental Legal Issues section at the beginning of this Memo, the Secretary's conclusion that § 7004 allows for *any* expansion of nonconforming uses if the statutory criteria are met is an overly broad, fundamental misstatement of the law. Expansions are subject to the limitations found in 7 Del. C. § 7003 and

[8] While the Order reaches this conclusion in connection with rejecting public comments based on § 4.6 of the CZA Regulations (which is covered in Ground # 3 below), the analysis applies with full force here because it deals with whether or not the transshipment amounts to a bulk product transfer facility.

[9] The Order claims that § 7002(b) defines bulk product transfer facility, Order at 6, but that is demonstrably wrong: § 7002(b) defines nonconforming use. The definition of bulk product transfer facility is found at § 7002(f).

the Section 4 Prohibitions. If the transshipment of ethanol under the Permit would create a new bulk product transfer facility, then the expansion is not allowed.

More fundamentally, however, the Secretary completely misreads the definition in § 7002(f), and particularly the second sentence. The first sentence defines a bulk product transfer facility as a docking facility that transfers bulk quantities of any substance from ship to shore and vice versa. The transfer of 10,000 bpd of ethanol from the Refinery's dock to barges and marine vessels under the Permit certainly fits that part of the definition. However, § 7002(f) expressly creates an important exception: "Not included in this definition is a docking facility or pier for a single industrial or manufacturing facility for which a permit is granted or which is a nonconforming use." This is sometimes called the "single industrial or manufacturing facility" exception. This Board, in one of its very first opinions under the Act, described what this exception means:

> It is quite clear that the Legislature did not intend that the exemption for a "docking facility or pier for a single industrial or manufacturing facility" should be used to subvert the purposes of the Coastal Zone Act. Rather, the Legislature intended to provide relief for industrial or manufacturing facilities which might find it desirable in the future to utilize a pier or dock as an integrated portion of the facility. The situation in which we would apply the "single facility" exemption might be illustrated as follows: The X Widget Company is located in the Coastal Zone adjacent to a Delaware waterway. X manufactures a widget composed primarily of plastic. Currently X ships and receives finished products and raw material by truck. The X management determines that the productive capacity of the plant and competitive factors require that X receive raw materials and ship finished product by water. This determination will require that X construct a docking facility. Such a facility is within the "single facility" exemption of the "bulk product transfer facility" prohibition. A similar exemption could be obtained by new facilities for which a Coastal Zone Permit has been granted. **The key to the exemption is that the "bulk product transfer facility" must be necessary for and utilized in the operation of the "single industrial or manufacturing facility.**"

Sun Oil Co. of Pennsylvania, Opinion at 6-7 (Coastal Zone Indust. Control Bd. November 29, 1972) (emphasis supplied).

In *Sun Oil*, this Board affirmed a decision of the State Planner which had found that a proposed pier expansion at Sun Oil's Marcus Hook facility extending into Delaware (and hence within the jurisdiction of the Coastal Zone Act) was prohibited as a new bulk product transfer facility. The pier had been used to off-load approximately 205,000 bpd of petroleum products for use at the refinery, of which approximately 180,000 bpd were used in refinery operations and approximately 18,000 bpd were received and then shipped without processing at the refinery (that is, transshipped). The pier expansion would be used to allow Sun Oil to increase transshipment volume to 300,000 bpd. *Id.* at 3,6. This Board found the proposed transshipment would amount to a prohibited bulk product transfer facility and that the single industrial or manufacturing facility exemption of § 7002(f) did not apply for two reasons.

The Board's first reason looked at the purpose behind the proposed use based on the transshipment volumes. The Board found that "the primary purpose of the pier at this time is to supply the Refinery," *Sun Oil* at 6, with only 18,000 bpd being transshipped. The Board stated that, with future transshipment volumes of 300,000 to 500,000 bpd compared to 180,000 bpd used in refinery operations,

> It is our opinion that Sun is attempting to use the existing incidental transshipment related to the Refinery as the basis of a subterfuge designed to circumvent the Coastal Zone Act. The most significant evidence on this point is that the new pier will act as a conduit for petroleum products rather than a facility necessary to the operation of the Refinery.

Id. The Board's second reason was that, given the legislative intent and key to the exemption set forth in the long quotation above, "[i]t is quite clear that the operation of the Marcus Hook Refinery is not dependent upon the operation of the pier as proposed by Sun," *id.* at 7-8, and the transshipment "is not an integral part of its current business of refining petroleum products." *Id.* at 9.

This Board's analysis in *Sun Oil* applies with full force here. In order for the "single industrial or manufacturing facility" exemption to apply, the Refinery must be able to show that the 10,000 bpd of ethanol are "necessary for and utilized in the operation of" the Refinery. As the Fundamental Facts set forth at the beginning of this Memo make clear, however, the 10,000 bpd of ethanol under the Permit are not going to be utilized in the operation of the Refinery at all (being above and beyond the 2,000 bpd the Refinery uses), but are being brought in so that they can be shipped out. Indeed, the transshipment of ethanol allowed under the Permit could take place even if the Refinery's petroleum refining operations were temporarily or permanently shut down. Quite simply, the excess ethanol is "not necessary for the operation of the Refinery" and is "not an integral part" of the Refinery's business of refining petroleum products. This is pure and simple transshipment of ethanol. Further, as the Board noted in *Sun Oil,* the fact that the volume of new petroleum products being brought in (300,000 – 500,000 bpd) was larger than the volume used by the Refinery (approximately 2-3 times larger) was "the most significant evidence" that "the new pier would act as a conduit for petroleum products rather than a facility necessary to the operation of the refinery." *Sun Oil* at 6. Here, the volume of ethanol being brought in for transshipment is **five times** the volume used by the Refinery in its operations. Thus, the "single industrial or manufacturing facility exemption" in § 7002(f)'s definition does not apply here.

The fact that the Refinery's pier may have "historically transferred petroleum related products," Order at 6-7—which is supported by nothing more in the administrative record than vague claims by the Refinery in its Application—does not alter this outcome. As the Board correctly noted in *Sun Oil*, prior shipments that supplied or were necessary to the operation of the Refinery are fundamentally different from transshipment. The Refinery seeks to engage in a new activity: to use its docking facility to load bulk qualities of ethanol manufactured elsewhere onto barges and marine vessels for the sole purpose of selling that ethanol to other customers. These bulk product transfers can happen without the Refinery doing any refining or even operating. To paraphrase this Board's language in *Sun Oil*, the Permit allows the Refinery to turn its pier into a "conduit for ethanol" that is not "necessary for the operation of the Refinery." Thus, the Permit allows the creation of a new bulk product transfer facility that was not in existence on June 28, 1971. Such a bulk product transfer facility is not allowed under 7 Del. C. § 7003 and § 4.5 of the CZA Regulations. As such, the Order and Permit were issued contrary to law. The Board should therefore reverse the Order and deny the Permit.

III. APPEAL GROUND #3: THE ORDER AND PERMIT VIOLATE 7 DEL. C. § 7003 AND SECTION 4.6 OF THE CZA REGULATIONS BECAUSE THEY ALLOW THE CONVERSION AND USE OF AN UNREGULATED OR EXEMPTED DOCKING FACILITY FOR THE TRANSFER OF BULK PRODUCTS (I.E., ETHANOL).

Consistent with the prohibition against new bulk product transfer facilities found in 7 Del. C. § 7003, § 4.6 of the CZA Regulations identifies "The conversion or use of existing unregulated, exempt, or permitted docking facilities for the transfer of bulk products" as one of the nine "uses or activities [] prohibited in the Coastal Zone" that are listed in the Section 4 Prohibitions. Appellants believe that the transshipment of ethanol allowed under the Permit violates these prohibitions.

As the Board's decision in *Sun Oil* suggests, a docking facility, when being utilized in and necessary for the operation of the Refinery, falls within the "single industry or manufacturing facility" exemption in the 7 Del. C. § 7002(f) definition of bulk product transfer facility. Appellants believe that the evidence will show that the Refinery's piers and docks—what the Order calls the Refinery's "integrated docking facility"—are "unregulated" and/or "exempt" from CZA regulation because they were are an integrated part of the Refinery's nonconforming heavy industry use as a refinery. Under the Permit, however, the use of the docks will change to acting as a "conduit" through which ethanol not processed by the Refinery is shipped out in bulk quantities. Therefore, the use of this "unregulated" and "exempt" docking facility to transfer bulk quantities of ethanol under the Permit violates the prohibition of § 4.6.

The Secretary attempts to avoid this conclusion by claiming that § 4.6 does not apply because "there is no 'conversion' or new 'use' of the facility . . . taking place." Order at 7. However, the Secretary contradicts himself when he admits that the docking facility must be changed (i.e., *converted*) to enable outgoing shipments of ethanol because there are only incoming shipments now. *Id.* This admission also proves that, while the docking facility is only being used for receipt of incoming shipments, it will be *used* for a new activity: "the transfer of bulk products" (10,000 bpd of ethanol). The transshipment of ethanol allowed under the permit therefore falls squarely within the language of the prohibition in § 4.6. As such, the Order and Permit were issued contrary to law. The Board should therefore reverse the Order and deny the Permit.

IV. APPEAL GROUND #4: THE SECRETARY FAILED TO CONSIDER ALL ENVIRONMENTAL IMPACTS AND EFFECTS ON NEIGHBORING LAND USES—SPECIFICALLY, THE ENVIRONMENTAL IMPACTS AND EFFECTS ON NEIGHBORING LAND USES OF SHIPPING ETHANOL TO THE FACILITY—AS REQUIRED BY 7 DEL. C. § 7004(B) AND THE SECTION 8.3.2 OF THE CZA REGULATIONS.

Section 7004(b) of the Act identifies six different "factors" that the Secretary and this Board "shall consider" when "passing on permit requests." The first of these factors relates to environmental impacts, which the Act describes in this way:

> Environmental impact, including but not limited to, probable air and water pollution likely to be generated by the proposed use under normal operating conditions as well as during mechanical malfunction and human error; likely destruction of wetlands and flora and fauna; impact of site preparation on

> drainage of the area in question, especially as it relates to flood control; impact of site preparation and facility operations on land erosion; effect of site preparation and facility operations on the quality and quantity of surface, ground and subsurface water resources, such as the use of water for processing, cooling, effluent removal, and other purposes; in addition, but not limited to, likelihood of generation of glare, heat, noise, vibration, radiation, electromagnetic interference and obnoxious odors.

7 Del. C. § 7004(b)(1). The fifth factor looks at neighboring land uses, which the Act describes in this way:

> Effect on neighboring land uses including, but not limited to, effect on public access to tidal waters, effect on recreational areas and effect on adjacent residential and agricultural areas.

7 Del. C. § 7004(b)(5). The fourth factor—"number and type of supporting facilities required and the impact of such facilities on all factors listed in this subsection," 7 Del. C. § 7004(b)(4), amplifies the first and fifth factors.[10] Section 8.3.2 of the CZA Regulations requires that the Secretary "shall consider" the six statutory factors, and amplifies the environmental impact factor by requiring the Secretary to consider "direct and cumulative environmental impacts."

The Secretary's Order makes no findings concerning any of the six factors; instead, it refers to the Technical Response Memorandum ("TRM") attached to the Order. The TRM claims that the only environmental impacts will be air emissions from loading ethanol at the piers, and claims that none of the other types of impacts specifically listed in § 7004(b)(1) will occur. TRM p. 2. However, the TRM analysis fails to discuss any of the following environmental impacts:

* air emissions from the barges/marine vessels that will be used to transport the

---

[10] The three other factors—which are not relevant to this appeal—are economic effect, 7 Del. C. § 7004(b)(2), aesthetic effect, *id.* at (b)(3), and zoning approval, *id.* at (b)(6).

transshipped ethanol from the Refinery to other customers.[11] Such vessels, operating in the Coastal Zone as they come to and leave from the Refinery's pier, will generate air pollution, but there is no consideration of that environmental effect evident in the TRM or the Secretary's analysis.

* noise from the barges/marine vessels that will be used to transport the transshipped ethanol from the Refinery to other customers. Such vessels, operating in the Coastal Zone as they come to and leave from the Refinery's pier, will generate noise, but there is no consideration of that environmental effect evident in the TRM or the Secretary's analysis.

* air emissions from the trains that bring ethanol to the Double Loop Track rail facility.[12] Diesel locomotives operating in the Coastal Zone as they come to and leave from the rail facility, will generate air pollution, but there is no consideration of that environmental effect evident in the TRM or the Secretary's analysis.

* noise from the trains that bring ethanol to the Double Loop Track rail facility. Diesel locomotives operating in the Coastal Zone as they come to and leave from the rail facility, will generate noise, but there is no consideration of that environmental effect evident in the TRM or the Secretary's analysis.

* Carbon dioxide emissions from the trains and barges/marine vessels as they come and go. Such CO_2 emissions contribute to climate change.

---

[11] While the language of the Refinery's public statements suggests that the primary if not sole method of importing the ethanol will be by rail, to the extent that the Refinery will bring some of the ethanol in by barge, then the emissions and noise from such *incoming* vessels are further environmental effects that the Secretary did not analyze.

[12] Consideration of the impacts from the trains is mandated by the fourth § 7004(b) factor. The trains and the Double Look Track are a "supporting facility" for the transshipment of ethanol because they are the way the ethanol gets to the Refinery (as noted above, the Refinery does not manufacture it) so that it can then be transshipped out on the barges/marine vessels.

Quite simply, the TRM (and therefore the Secretary's) analysis of environmental effects is incomplete.

On the issue of effects on neighboring land uses, the TRM claims (incorrectly) that the proposed facility is "within the footprint of the existing nonconforming use," and makes the conclusory statement that "effects on neighboring uses will be minimal." TRM p. 2. However, the TRM fails to discuss any of the following potential effects on neighboring uses:

* effects of air pollution and noise on Delaware City and surrounding areas from the barges/marine vessels that will be used to transport the transshipped ethanol from the Refinery to other customers.
* effects of air pollution and noise on residential areas from the trains that bring ethanol to the Double Loop Track rail facility.

Quite simply, the TRM (and therefore the Secretary's) analysis of effects on neighboring land uses is incomplete.

The failure to consider and analyze these environmental and neighboring land use effects undermines the Secretary's entire decision. Section 9.1.1 of the CZA Regulations requires that

> Any application for a Coastal Zone permit for an activity or facility that will result in any negative environmental impact shall contain an offset proposal. Offset proposals must more than offset the negative environmental impacts associated with the proposed project or activity requiring a permit.

By focusing solely on air emissions from the loading ethanol at the piers, the Secretary approved an Offset Proposal that deals solely with those emissions. If, however, the emissions from marine vessels and trains are included, the Offset Proposal may not "more than offset the negative environmental impacts associated with the proposed project" of transshipping 10,000 bpd of ethanol. Further, the Offset Proposal's purported reduction of emissions at the Refinery's Truck Rack would do absolutely nothing to address—much less "more than offset"—the noise generated by the barges, marine vessels, and trains. In short, the Secretary's analysis is incomplete, and the Offset Proposal may not satisfy the requirements of the CZA Regulations. The Board should reverse the Order and deny the Permit.[13]

V. APPEAL GROUND #5: THE SECRETARY FAILED TO CONSIDER ANY IMPACTS OF THE PROPOSED ETHANOL TRANSFER ACTIVITY ON THE DEPARTMENT'S ENVIRONMENTAL GOALS FOR THE COASTAL ZONE AND THE ENVIRONMENTAL INDICATORS USED TO ASSESS LONG-TERM ENVIRONMENTAL QUALITY WITHIN THE ZONE AS REQUIRED BY THE SECTION 8.3.3 OF THE CZA REGULATIONS.

Section 8.3 of the CZA Regulations specifies what the Secretary and DNREC must do in reviewing applications for CZA Permits. Section 8.3.3 imposes the following mandatory duty:

> The Secretary shall also consider any impacts the proposed activity may have on the Department's environmental goals for the Coastal Zone and the environmental indicators used to assess long-term environmental quality within the zone.

A review of the 10/26/16 Environmental Assessment signed by the Secretary, the Order, and the TRM shows absolutely no discussion (and therefore no consideration) of impacts from the proposed transshipment of ethanol on "the Department's environmental goals for the Coastal Zone" or on "the environmental indicators used to assess long-term environmental quality within the zone." Appellants believe the evidence will show that, while the Department may have at one time adopted "environmental goals," DNREC has never adopted "environmental indicators." This is despite the fact that the Department stated that:

> DNREC will develop within 12 months of the ratification of the Coastal Zone MOU[which happened in 1999], a set of Coastal Zone environmental goals and appropriate environmental indicators which will highlight the most significant challenges to the Coastal Zone; and

[13] Appellants recognize that, while the Board has the power to modify, deny, or affirm issuance of the Permit, 7 Del. C. § 7006, it does not have the power to remand the Permit back to DNREC for further analysis—what is the most obvious remedy for what the Secretary and DNREC failed to do when issuing the Permit. For this and Grounds # 5 – 7, in lieu of asking the Board to fix the Secretary's failures via modifying the Permit (which would be an arduous task given the lack of proof necessary for the Board to determine what would be appropriate modifications), the Appellants instead urge denial of the Permit. If the Refinery wants to reapply, and have the shortcomings addressed in a new permitting process, it and DNREC can do so.

> DNREC is responsible for defining, prioritizing, and making a matter of public record the set of goals and indicators for assessing the environmental quality in the Coastal Zone. Once goals for Coastal Zone have been established, DNREC will select a detailed set of indicators for use in assessing the quality of the environment as measured against those goals, and to monitor progress over time.

§§ 3.1, 3.2 of Appendix C to the CZA Regulations The environmental indicators are supposed to be important to the administration of the Coastal Zone Act. As DNREC has stated:

> The indicators will serve several important purposes. First, they will assist NREC in developing a more accurate picture of the environmental quality of the Coastal Zone, and measuring trends in this quality over time. Second, they will assist DNREC and project applicants by providing a means for evaluating the potential impacts of proposed changes in facility operations and proposed offsets on the Coastal Zone environment.

§ 3.1 of Appendix C to the CZA Regulations.

Section 8.3.3 of the CZA Regulations required the Secretary to consider the impacts of the proposed transshipment of ethanol on DNREC's environmental goals and environmental indicators. The record will show that no such consideration took place as to any existent goals and could not have taken place for the non-existent environmental indicators. As such, the Secretary failed to comply with the mandatory requirements of the CZA Regulations, and therefore the Permit was issued in violation of and contrary to the law. The Board should reverse the Order and deny the Permit.

VI. APPEAL GROUND #6: THE SECRETARY FAILED TO USE A SET OF PRIORITIZED ENVIRONMENTAL INDICATORS AS A TOOL FOR ASSESSING ENVIRONMENTAL IMPACTS AS REQUIRED BY SECTIONS 5.3 AND 5.4 OF THE DNREC GUIDANCE FOUND AT "APPENDIX C TO THE REGULATIONS GOVERNING DELAWARE'S COASTAL ZONE."

The Order and Permit make clear that part of the analysis for the Permit included consideration of an Offset Proposal supposedly designed to offset the air emissions from the loading of ethanol onto barges for shipment. Section 5.0 of the DNREC Guidance found at

Appendix C to the CZA Regulations sets forth the details of how the Secretary and DNREC will evaluate offset proposals.[14] Sections 5.3 and 5.4 impose these requirements on the Secretary's evaluation of offsets:

> 5.3 The Secretary shall make decisions on applicants' status decision requests and environmental impact assessments, in writing, based on all of the expected environmental impacts of the total project on the health of the Coastal Zone, including both positive and negative impacts. Impacts may be related to air and water emissions, or they may be related to other factors such as the viability of wildlife habitat, the protection of wetlands, or the creation or preservation of open space. **The Secretary will develop and use a set of prioritized environmental indicators as a tool for assisting these determinations as discussed elsewhere in this guidance.**
>
> 5.4 **The Secretary shall consider likely cumulative impacts of proposed activities on the environment and the relevant environmental indicators.** The Secretary shall also give consideration to the potential for negative cumulative impacts in situations where cross-media offsets are proposed.

(emphasis supplied). As noted above, Appellants believe the evidence will show that DNREC has never created any environmental indicators under the Coastal Zone Act. Thus, the Secretary failed to comply with the requirements of §§ 5.3 and 5.4 of the DNREC Guidance found at Appendix C to the CZA Regulations, and therefore the Permit was issued in violation of and contrary to the law. The Board should reverse the Order and deny the Permit.

[14] Appellants recognize that—as pointed out during the discussion of the Secretary's reliance on § 1.2 of Appendix C in the Fundamental Legal Issues at the beginning of this Memo—the provisions of the DNREC Guidance found in Appendix C are not regulation and do not have the force of law. However, § 1.4 makes clear that the Guidance "is made available to interested citizens and applicants to better understand how these regulations will be interpreted and implemented by the Department," and the Guidance gives way only when there is a conflict with the CZA Regulations themselves (like the conflict between § 1.2 of Appendix C. and the Section 4 Prohibitions found in the CZA Regulations). In Appeal Grounds #6 and #7, there is no conflict between the Appendix C sections cited and the Regulations, and so the Secretary was bound to follow how DNREC has said it will interpret and implement the Coastal Zone Act program.

VII. APPEAL GROUND #7: THE SECRETARY FAILED TO INCLUDE WELL-DEFINED AND MEASURABLE COMMITMENTS OR ACCOMPLISHMENTS CONCERNING THE PROPOSED OFFSET PROPOSAL THAT ARE INDEPENDENTLY AUDITABLE BY THE DEPARTMENT AND AVAILABLE TO THE PUBLIC VIA THE FREEDOM OF INFORMATION ACT AND FAILED TO INCLUDE INSPECTION, REPORTING AND NOTIFICATION OBLIGATIONS IN THE PERMIT CONCERNING THE OFFSET PROPOSAL AS REQUIRED BY SECTION 5.8 OF THE DNREC GUIDANCE FOUND AT "APPENDIX C TO THE REGULATIONS GOVERNING DELAWARE'S COASTAL ZONE."

The Order refers to, and the Permit imposes, a requirement to undertake the Offset Proposal contained in the Refinery's Permit Application. According to the Order:

> For the reasons set forth in the Secretary's Environmental Assessment dated September 28, 2016, the Department finds that the total anticipated increase in fugitive volatile organic compound ("VOC") emissions (0.8 tons per year) will be more than offset by the installation of a new vapor capture system at the trucking terminal that will result in the reduction of VOCs by 1.1 tons per year.

Order at p. 8. Setting aside the issue of the completeness of the Secretary's analysis of negative environmental impacts (*see* Ground #4 above), it is clear that the Permit only requires that the Offset Proposal (the vapor capture system) be installed. The Permit contains no provision which will ensure that the Offset in fact produces a 1.1 ton reduction of VOC emissions or that the Offset's reductions are in fact greater than the VOC emissions generated by the ethanol transshipment operation under the Permit. In effect, the Secretary simply accepted the Refinery's claims in the Application. This fails to meet DNREC's own Guidance.

Section 5.8 of the DNREC Guidance found at Appendix C to the CZA Regulations states:

> All offset projects must be incorporated into the Coastal Zone permit as an enforceable condition of the permit. Since some of the benefits of "flexibility" are achieved immediately upon issuance of the permit (i.e., permission to proceed), and most benefits of "environmental improvement" are achieved over time, **the permit itself must include well-defined and measurable commitments or accomplishments which are independently auditable by the Department, and available to the public via the Freedom of information Act (FOIA). DNREC will also provide inspection, reporting and/or notification obligations in the permit depending on the company's compliance record and the nature of the offset project** (emphasis supplied).

Here, the Permit lacks any "well-defined and measurable commitments or accomplishments which are independently auditable" by DNREC and available to the public via FOIA such as monitoring and reporting requirements which would prove the annual 1.1 ton VOC reduction that the Refinery claims and which DNREC relies upon to find an offset of negative environmental effects. As § 5.8 makes clear, DNREC can and "will provide" such reporting requirements in the permit—especially in light of the Refinery's compliance record that includes violations of the Secretary's May 31, 2013 Order limiting crude oil shipments to the Paulsboro, NJ refinery and the Refinery's repeated and continued air pollution releases and air permit violations.

Because the Permit fails to include monitoring and reporting requirements to ensure that the environmental benefits of the Offset Proposal are in fact achieved, it does not comply with § 5.8 of the DNREC Guidance found at Appendix C to the CZA Regulations, and therefore the Permit was issued in violation of and contrary to the law. The Board should reverse the Order and deny the Permit.

CONCLUSION

For the reasons set forth above, Appellants Delaware Audubon Society and League of Women Voters of Delaware respectfully request that the Coastal Zone Industrial Control Board reverse Order No. 2016-CZ-0050 and deny Coastal Zone Act Permit No. 427P, and for such other relief as the Board deems just and proper.

Respectfully submitted,

DELAWARE AUDUBON and
LEAGUE OF WOMEN VOTERS OF DELAWARE

By: ____/s/ Kenneth T. Kristl__________
Kenneth T. Kristl, Esq. (DE Bar # 5200)
Environmental & Natural Resources Law Clinic
Widener University Delaware Law School
4601 Concord Pike
Wilmington, DE 19803
(302) 477-2053
(302) 477-2032 (fax)
ktkristl@widener.edu

Counsel for Appellants

CERTIFICATE OF SERVICE

The undersigned, an attorney, hereby certifies that he caused a copy of the foregoing **APPELLANTS' PRE-HEARING MEMO/STATEMENT OF LEGAL ISSUES** and the **APPENDIX TO APPELLANTS' PRE-HEARING MEMO/STATEMENT OF LEGAL ISSUES** to be served upon the following persons:

Lisa Johannsen
Administrative Assistant
Coastal Zone Industrial Control Board
Department of Natural Resources and Environmental Control
89 Kings Highway
Dover, DE 19901
302-739-9000
Lisa.johannsen@state.de.us

Frank Broujos
Deputy Attorney General
Department of Justice
820 North French Street
6th Floor
Wilmington, DE
302-577-8940
Frank.broujos@state.de.us
Counsel for the Coastal Zone Industrial Control Board

Max Walton, Esq.
Matthew Boyer, Esq.
Connolly Gallagher LLP
267 East Main Street
Newark, DE 19711
302-888-6297
mwalton@connollygallagher.com, mboyer@connollygallagher.com
Counsel for the Department of Natural Resources and Environmental Control

Joseph C. Schoell, Esq.
Drinker Biddle & Reath LLP
222 Delaware Avenue Suite 1410
Wilmington, DE 19801
(302) 467-4245
Joseph.schoell@dbr.com
Counsel for the Delaware City Refining Company

Bart E. Cassidy, Esq.
Katherine Vaccaro, Esq.
Stephan Daly, Esq.
Manko Gold Katcher & Fox, LLP
401 City Avenue, Suite 901
Bala Cynwyd, PA 19004
484-430-2306
bcassidy@mankogold.com, kvaccaro@mankogold.com, sdaly@mankogold.com
Counsel for the Delaware City Refining Company

by email and by overnight messenger sent this 30th day of January, 2017.

By: /s/ Kenneth T. Kristl
Kenneth T. Kristl, Esq. (DE Bar # 5200)
Environmental & Natural Resources Law Clinic
Widener University Delaware Law School
4601 Concord Pike
Wilmington, DE 19803
(302) 477-2053
(302) 477-2032 (fax)
ktkristl@widener.edu

Counsel for Appellants

APPENDIX TAB 8

Annotations Follow Notice of Appeal Document

SUPERIOR COURT OF THE STATE OF DELAWARE

KEEP OUR WELLS CLEAN, GAIL SALOMON, EUGENIA GRACE NAVITSKI, VLAD ERIC NAVITSKI, THOMAS DIORIO, LYNN TAYLOR-MILLER, CHARLIE MILLER, and VIRGINIA WEEKS,	)
Appellants,	)
	)
v.	) **C.A. No.**
	)
DEPARTMENT OF NATURAL RESOURCES AND ENVIRONMENTAL CONTROL, ARTESIAN WASTEWATER MANAGEMENT, INC,	) **Appeal from June 10, 2019 Decision and Final Order of the Environmental Appeals Board, Case No. 2017-14**
Appellees.	)

<u>NOTICE OF APPEAL</u>

Keep Our Wells Clean, Gail Salomon, Eugenia Grace Navitski (f/k/a Yauheniya Zialenskaya), Vlad Eric Navitiski (f/k/a Uladzislau I. Navitski), Thomas Diorio, Lynn Taylor-Miller, Charlie Miller, and Virginia Weeks (collectively, "Appellants"), pursuant to 7 *Del. C.* § 6009 and Rule 72 of the Rules of the Superior Court, hereby appeal the May 22, 2018 decision on the Appellants' Motions in *Limine* and the June 10, 2019 Decision and Final Order of the Environmental Appeals Board ("Board") dismissing its appeal of Secretary's Order No. 2017-W-0029 by the Secretary of the Department of Natural Resources and Environmental Control (DNREC). In support thereof, Appellants state as follows:

1. On November 2, 2017, the Secretary of the Department of Natural Resources and Environmental Control issued Secretary's Order No. 2017-W-0029 approving Artesian Wastewater Management, Inc.'s Application to Amend the Construction Permit for Phase 1 of the Artesian Northern Sussex Regional Water Recharge Facility near Milton, Sussex County. The original permit, granted under Secretary's Order No. 2012-W-0052, issued March 12, 2013 was being amended to permit the facility to serve a single commercial/industrial customer, Allen Harim,

LLC with wastewater services for up to 2.0 million gallons per day of industrial wastewater from its Harbeson, Delaware poultry processing facility.

2. Appellants appealed the Secretary's Order to the Board pursuant to 7 *Del. C.* § 6008.

3. On May 22, 2018 the Board held a public hearing on Appellees' Motions to Dismiss and in *Limine.* After consideration of the parties' arguments, the Motions to Dismiss filed by DNREC and Artesian challenging the Appellants' standing were denied.[1] The Board then considered the two Motions in *Limine* and granted them "such that evidence presented must be limited to evidence before the Secretary that speaks to proper site selection and system design and not the operations of the plant."[2] The May 22, 2018 ruling on the Motions *in Limine* was not a final order in that it did not dispose of the case and the Board never issued a written decision as required for final decisions under the Administrative Procedures Act.

4. On March 12, 2019, The Board conducted a public hearing on the merits of the appeal. At that hearing, the Board voted to dismiss the appeal and affirm the Secretary's November 2, 2017 Order. The June 10, 2019 Decision and Final Order sets forth the Board's reasoning and analysis. It makes final and appealable both the May 22, 2018 decision on the Motions *in Limine* and the Board's disposition of the merits of the appeal itself.

5. Appellants are filing this appeal within 30 days of the Opinion and Final Order as required under 7 *Del. C.* § 6009.

6. Appellants, as the parties who filed the appeal and participated in the public hearings, and because Keep Our Wells Clean's members' and the individual Appellants' aesthetic, recreational, health and other interests will be adversely affected by the Board's decisions and the underlying Amended Permit approved in the Secretary's Order, are persons aggrieved by the Board's May 22, 2018 and June 10, 2019 Decisions and Final Order and therefore entitled to appeal pursuant to 7 *Del. C.* § 6009.

7. The Board's May 22, 2018 decisions on the Motions in *Limine* and the June 10, 2019 Decision and Final Order are arbitrary, capricious, an abuse of

[1] Transcript of May 22, 2018 Hearing, 110

[2] *Id.* at 167.

discretion, contrary to law, and otherwise illegal in their limitation of the evidence to be presented and denial of the appeal of the Secretary's Order in that the Board improperly ignored, misinterpreted, and/or misapplied the factual record of, and the applicable Delaware law governing, this matter.

WHEREFORE, Appellants Keep Our Wells Clean, Gail Salomon, Yauheniya Zialenskaya, Uladzislau I. Navitski, Thomas Diorio, Lynn Taylor-Miller, Charlie Miller, and Virginia Weeks respectfully request that this Court reverse the May 22, 2018 decision on the Appellants' Motions in *Limine* and the June 10, 2019 Decision and Final Order of the Environmental Appeals Board and remand the matter back to the Board for consideration of the merits of the appeal.

Respectfully submitted,

Keep Our Wells Clean, Gail Salomon, Yauheniya Zialenskaya, Uladzislau I. Navitski, Thomas Diorio, Lynn Taylor-Miller, Charlie Miller, and Virginia Weeks

By: /s/ Kenneth T. Kristl

KENNETH T. KRISTL, ESQ. (DE Bar #5200)
Environmental & Natural Resources Law Clinic
Widener University Delaware Law School
4601 Concord Pike
Wilmington, DE 19803
Ph: (302) 477-2053
Fx: (302) 477-2032
ktkristl@widener.edu

Counsel for Appellants

Made in United States
Orlando, FL
05 November 2026

90230137R00118